The Secret World
of Day Laborers

DICK J. REAVIS

CATCHING
OUT

SIMON & SCHUSTER
New York   London   Toronto   Sydney

Simon & Schuster
1230 Avenue of the Americas
New York, NY 10020

First Simon & Schuster hardcover edition February 2010

SIMON & SCHUSTER and colophon are registered
trademarks of Simon & Schuster, Inc.

For information about special discounts for bulk purchases,
please contact Simon & Schuster Special Sales at
1-866-506-1949 or business@simonandschuster.com.

The Simon & Schuster Speakers Bureau can bring authors
to your live event. For more information or to book an event,
contact the Simon & Schuster Speakers Bureau at
1-866-248-3049 or visit our website at www.simonspeakers.com.

Designed by Jill Putorti

Manufactured in the United States of America

10   9   8   7   6   5   4   3   2   1

Library of Congress Cataloging-in-Publication Data
Reavis, Dick J.
Catching out : the secret world of day laborers / Dick J. Reavis
   p. cm.
Includes index.
1. Day laborers—United States. I. Title.
HD5854.2.U6R43   2010
331.5'44—dc22   2009023779

ISBN 978-1-4391-5480-9

To my wife, Miriam Lizcano, who has put up with me,
and to John Stanford of San Antonio, who set an example of decency

Contents

CATCHING OUT

THE PROJECT

I am sixty-three. For thirty years I was a carefree, adventuresome, and stubborn reporter. Seeing retirement on the horizon, I left journalism five years ago for an academic job that came with a defined-benefit retirement plan. But since Social Security and the retirement pension that I'll receive won't save me from want, two years ago, even before clouds appeared on the nation's economic horizon, I began to look for ways to supplement my old-age income.

Working as a Walmart greeter is not for me. I am temperamentally and philosophically unfit for a role as Mr. Nice. But for a guy whose résumé admits to only journalistic and academic jobs, I've always known more than I should about blue-collar work because I grew up around it.

Fifty years ago, people applied for Social Security cards, not through their parents, as infants, but when they entered the labor market. I got my Social Security card at twelve when I became a part-time printer's helper. From then until I graduated from high school, I worked twenty to thirty hours a week as a stereotyper, a "stuffer" and "swamper"—doing unskilled and semiskilled tasks in the letterpress trade. In college and for a couple of years afterward I skipped from job to job, sometimes finding work through day-labor halls—businesses that hire every morning and pay at the end of each workday.

I was briefly a "gum boy" in a San Francisco envelope factory and, for more than a year, the operator of a Ludlow machine—a piece of printing-industry equipment—in a New Orleans stamp and stencil shop. On sojourns at day labor, I helped install posts for electrical lines, spray-painted headboards in a furniture factory, and hung spun glass insulation—without a safety mask—in office buildings under construction.

Day-labor jobs and their ambience suited me. Conditions weren't often onerous and labor-management relations were as they should be. I didn't have to intone, "Good morning! How are your kids?" Nobody asked me to attend departmental picnics, go to lunch with a supervisor, or contribute to the United Way.

On day-labor jobs, my superiors expected me to despise, even ridicule, them and their superiors. Sometimes they browbeat me and other casuals, but they didn't persist, probably because they didn't have to put up with us for more than a couple of days, maybe because they believed that we were carrying switchblade knives.

But if day labor was usually a pleasure, it was a puzzlement too. One of the lingering, troubling impressions that I carried away from sampling the world of labor was that in nonunion shops, American workers and their employers rarely engage in frank or open talk about labor-management affairs. Instead, workers deceive, and employers abuse, in silent and faceless ways.

For example, while I was working on a swing or evening shift in a printing plant, a couple of regular employees telephoned me two or three nights a week, asking me to punch their time cards for them; they didn't present themselves for work until an hour or even ninety minutes later. They expected me to help them cheat the company, and of course, I did.

In the envelope plant where I worked, the banging, roar, and groaning of cutters, punches, and presses was overwhelming. Foremen and the plant superintendent, despite having offices in a glassed-in second-story space, were aware of the racket and the irritation it caused. Veteran workers prescribed a remedy—at least one beer every hour. Earplugs were almost unknown in those days, but the beer prescription worked: It turned the din into white noise, like the sound of a waterfall. Our superiors knew that we were drinking, but looked the other way, because on accounting books, beer paid for by workers was cheaper than insulating the plant at company expense. Nobody was ever fired for drinking except a shipping clerk who one night put a case of beer on his desk and ceremoniously got bombed while refusing to ship a single box.

For more than a week in the mid-nineties I worked a day-labor job at a plant that recycled telephone cables. In a building that I never saw, machines ground the cables to a pulp, then augured them through basins of water: The copper from the lines dropped out, while bits of wet plastic sheathing were augured through a long steel box, through the room where I worked and to a collection point outdoors. The augur made a ninety-degree bend on its way outside, and at the turn, it sometimes jammed. Engineers or workers at the plant had removed the cover on its steel box, about three feet on each side of the turn. My job was to stand at the bend with a stick, poking the plastic particles to keep them moving through the augur.

On my first afternoon, I realized that a safety engineer would consider my job unsafe: If I slipped while standing over the augur box, to brace my fall I might stick my hand inside the box—and lose it. After a couple of days, I telephoned the regional office of the Occupational Safety and Health Administration (OSHA) to inquire about the legality of that jury-rig. The agent on the other end of the line told me that "an open augur is always illegal," but that if I filed a complaint, it would be six weeks before his office could inspect the workplace. I quit the job the following morning, not because I was afraid of the augur, but because I was assigned to the job alone. One of the pleasures of labor is the companionship of the work gang, but the augur job gave me solitude instead.

I didn't always know what to think of the sneaking, cheating, and abuses that I saw, except that it would have been better if all of us, workers and bosses, had hashed things out in open discussion. I am still perplexed by a scene I witnessed at a chemical plant where I worked as a day laborer. An older man among the regular employees had gone blind a month or two before he would have vested in the company's retirement plan. He and his coworkers decided to keep his sightlessness secret. They brought him to the plant each morning and briskly ushered him to the shed where the maintenance crew gathered. They'd then walk him to task after task on the plant grounds, handing him a shovel or rake or pick or hose, and tell him where he was and what he should pretend to be doing. One of his comrades usually stood near, to warn him if higher-ups were coming. Two or three times, lookout duty fell to me, and I, of course, felt honored to be his watchman.

When I began to toy with the idea of returning to "casual" labor with retirement in view, like any American with a computer and a library card, I tried to see if I could update my savvy by reading. Mostly, I drew blanks. No popular works about day-labor agencies are in print except for two, both from academic presses—and both about day labor in Tokyo! Government reports weren't much help either. The most recent was a 2002 review from the General Accounting Office, which found that "little is actually known about who these day laborers are, what their working conditions are, or the extent to which protections afforded under federal wage and safety laws are enforced."

Sociologists have published more than a dozen studies, but the most thorough of them focus on casual laborers who are undocumented immigrants, the kind of workers who stand on street corners or outside home improvement stores, who negotiate wages while standing at the windows of pickup trucks—and who face dangers and deceptions that no citizen would endure. A few scholarly studies review day labor in the context of homelessness or parole from prisons, both overlapping but distinct problems. Perhaps more important, all of the sociologists I read gathered their information from surveys and interviews. What they report is only as reliable as its self-interested sources.

The chief thing that I learned from the literature was that as few as eight hundred thousand and as many as two million workers, mostly men, show up at labor halls every day. I figured that despite my age, I could still slip into a crowd that big. After all, day labor is a very American occupation. Its workers are relatively nameless and rootless, and my observation has been that day to day, nothing—not climate, nor family, nor place, nor religion, nor ideology, nor fealty of any kind—really identifies or unites the disparate strands of our nation, nothing except work, pop culture, and pay. And in labor halls, nobody talks of anything else.

The work-centeredness of American life, however, as sociologists have for decades reported, is as much a social as an economic bond. Workers on any job form friendships, even if they hate their jobs and on paydays, despair. The upshot of this, for me, was that like it or not, if I returned to day-labor chores, I had to expect that I'd long for acceptance among my peers, and be judged by them. I wasn't sure that I could make the grade.

One specter that gnawed at me was my lack of fitness, largely because the unwritten rule of blue-collar workplaces is "Carry your end of the load." I have a touch of chronic obstructive pulmonary disease, or COPD, my reward for thirty-five years of three-pack-a-day smoking as a younger man. Under exertion I sometimes get winded and have to stop moving to catch my breath.

One Monday halfway through the first of my two summers of day-labor reprise, to my surprise I awoke with severe pain in my right knee. I was unable to walk without a cane. Promptly I consulted a series of orthopedists and therapists, whose consistent advice to me was, "You are an old man. You have arthritis. Get used to it." Ultimately my general practitioner prescribed a nonnarcotic painkiller that, when taken in conjunction with a medication to prevent the painkiller from giving me an ulcer, allowed me to return to my feet. But every day afterward I feared drawing work assignments that I couldn't perform.

My experience told me that if I refused or walked off a job, I probably wouldn't be fired by a day-labor agency, not because any law truly shields the infirm, but because even the youngest muscle-workers have a hidden disability: if not lungs, then backs or shoulders or knees—or homelessness, or drug or alcohol dependency. One of the reasons that people turn to day-labor halls is that, for one reason or another, they've become unable to keep grueling forty-hour schedules.

Whether or not my coworkers would accept me with my frailties, I could not foresee. In my prior jobs as a blue-collar man, I had always been an outlier, a passerby, not an accepted member of a group. On the one job where I had remained long enough to be judged—at the New Orleans stamp and stencil shop—I'd failed the test. On my last day, before departing, without saying so for a white-collar debut, my foreman, Pete, who had barked at, but never really spoken to me, took the opportunity to say something. He told me what he really thought:

"Boy, there's something wrong with you," he'd spat. "You sit there at lunch, just reading, reading. I can see reading if you've got to figure out how to do something. But reading just to read, that don't make no sense."

With my retirement in view, I signed on at a labor hall despite old anxieties about my chances of social integration. I did not warn my new employers or my coworkers about my infirmities, nor did I tell them that I owned a car. Fortunately, nobody asked about my employment background. I rode to work on a bicycle, which, because the hall provided no place for locking it, I parked in a rack a few blocks away.

On my first day, I was dispatched to a job.

This volume is an account of what I saw, heard, and thought during my months as a temporary working stiff in an economy headed for decline.

2

THE HOLE

Lester and I were facing each other on opposite sides of the hole, which was about eighteen inches deep and eighteen inches in diameter. He had a mattock, a tool that everyone today calls a pickax. I had a spade. Our job was to widen the hole to a diameter of about three feet.

Lester was a guy I'd seen various times at the labor hall from which we worked, an average-sized man, maybe five foot nine, weighing about 175 pounds.[*] He had an angelic, benevolent face and was always dressed in like-new slacks and button-down shirts, not in the scruffy T-shirt-and-jeans attire of his peers.

As dark as coffee, he was in his forties and balding. Wrinkles seemed to have formed his face into a permanent grin. He kept to himself, always smiling. I don't think I'd heard him speak before that morning.

As he swung his pickax, I noticed that his aim was off the mark. The instrument's blade was falling about four inches away from the hole, and not, as it should have been, an inch or two from its border.

---

[*] Note to the reader: To avoid embarrassing my subjects and to discourage harassment suits, I have changed the names of the people and firms mentioned in all but the final chapter.

He was making stab marks in the ground, but dirt wasn't falling into the hole.

I watched for a few seconds. His eyes were on the pickax, but he hadn't noticed that he was too far from the hole's edge.

Dolly, the dispatcher at the labor hall, had warned me, I suppose. When she offered me the job, she'd told me, "Look out for Lester, will you? He can't see too well. You may have to guide him."

Dolly—a rosy-cheeked, pudgy, unfailingly friendly white woman in her late twenties—had told me that the job was "moving trees." I didn't know what that might involve. I had asked her.

"Don't worry, I've sent you to worse," she said.

On my way out, I'd also asked Milton Johnson, a slender, fiftyish, jet-black man, one of the hall's old-timers, what "moving trees" might mean.

"Moving trees? Well, the time I did it, it was like, they have all of these branches cut up," Johnson said. "Somebody has already cut them with a chain saw. You have to pick them up and throw them in a back-hoe. It ain't too bad."

But as it had turned out, "moving trees" this time meant digging, one of the tasks that day laborers abhor.

The boss man, a thirtyish white guy with blond hair, wraparound sunglasses, short pants, and a baseball hat, came to the spot where we were digging. He was dragging a water hose. He directed its stream into the hole, to soften the ground. Lester and I backed away, and when we did, I sidled over and in a whisper offered to exchange tools. He happily took my shovel, and when the boss man went off, Lester began digging—at the edge of the hole. But I noticed that to find the hole, he first placed the spade inside, then pulled it toward him until he touched its edge. He was finding it more by feel than by sight.

The excavation wasn't taxing—the ground was fairly soft—and it took less than an hour to expand the hole to size. The boss man checked our work with a tape measure and said we were done.

We had been digging at the margin of a yard in a suburban housing development that, from the looks of things, had been built about ten years earlier. On the edge of the yard adjoining us stood a crepe myrtle tree, perhaps twelve feet tall. Our next chore, the boss man said, was to unearth the tree and move it into the hole that we had dug.

The occupant of the adjacent house was planning to move, and was giving the crepe myrtle to his neighbor, the boss man's client. The boss man owned a tree-moving service, literally that: His business card carried the words "Tree Moving Service."

We had to pick and dig a narrow trench around the tree so that we could lift or pull it out of the ground. The ground sloped, and its downside was thick with roots that were tough to cut. About half an hour after we'd begun, having scraped out a trench, we rocked the tree. But it wouldn't budge. Though our trench had cut the visible roots, we now had to dig beneath the tree as best we could. It was slow going. Lester used his garden spade. I got the other available spade, a post-hole digger. We went to our knees, shoved and hacked, cutting the roots that we struck.

The boss man brought a long length of nylon webbing, about an inch wide. We formed a file, each of us holding a length of the webbing above our heads. Then we walked around the tree, wrapping its branches inside the circle we made. The boss man had us bring a stepladder from his pickup, and standing on it, he tied a special knot in the webbing, then had us go around again, and again, lowering our arms with each circuit. We were compressing the tree's branches, folding them toward the centerline formed by its trunk. This was to make the tree easier to move to the hole, the boss man said.

From its base, we rocked the tree again, and it began to yield. About this time, the client came up. He was dressed like the boss man, in a baseball cap, polo shirt, shorts, and jogging shoes; I noticed the initials of a collegiate social fraternity tattooed on his left ankle. He joined in the back-and-forthing. The tree gave way, tumbled atop the client, and swept the cap off his head. We lifted the tree off him and he crawled out, waving his cap. He was a little scratched, but essentially unhurt.

"Whatever happened to teenagers?" I quipped.

"Huh! They don't do work like this anymore," he said.

Two weeks later, I read a newspaper report about a study by the National Institute of Child Health and Human Development. It found that "while 90 percent of 9-year-olds get a couple of hours of exercise most days, fewer than 3 percent of 15-year-olds do." Old men do the lifting and the digging, the story said.

Once we had the tree on the ground, the job was easy. On one end, it was a ball of roots and clay, chest high. On the other, it was a sheaf of bound branches, waist high. I pushed the ball, as if it were a chariot wheel, to make it roll, while the boss man and Lester held on to its branches to keep them from pivoting. Within minutes we had rolled the tree into the hole we'd dug, pushed it upright, packed dirt around its edges, untied its webbing, and tied its trunk to four lines of webbing that ran to stakes we had hammered into the ground.

We finished a little past noon. The boss told us to put his tools into the bed of his pickup, gather our belongings, and get inside its cab. Then he went to talk to the client, who was waiting in his driveway, twenty yards from the pickup.

Lester's backpack was in plain view, next to mine, at a spot near the boundary between the two yards, not more than ten feet from the pickup's cab. But he wandered. He went walking even to the front porch of the client's yard. The client was writing a check. He and the boss man didn't notice.

I called to Lester. He heard me, but had to stop and scan, craning his neck to find me. I should have been visible on his left. He had a dead eye, it seemed.

"It's over here!" I called out. I was leaning on the hood of the cab, sipping a lukewarm Pepsi that I'd brought.

Lester began walking in my direction. He came within ten feet of his backpack, but still didn't see it.

"Turn around and look down at your feet," I called again.

He stopped, scanned the ground, picked up his backpack, and ambled to the cab.

When he'd finished his business, the boss man came to the pickup, followed by his client who—thoughtful fellow!—brought ten- or twelve-ounce bottles of water in his hands. He gave one to each of us. They were welcome and cold.

We were half-expecting the boss man to say that we were done for the day, and neither of us would have minded. Digging is hard work, and at Labor-4-U and most halls, workers are guaranteed that even if they complete a job in less time, they'll get four hours' pay.

But once we were in the pickup, the boss man didn't offer to drive us back to where he'd met us, nor did he even mention lunch. Instead, he started his engine and said that he had another chore, "similar to the one you just did."

He drove into the countryside, onto a dirt road that ran by a farmhouse that he said belonged to his parents. In a clearing leading into a field, I saw a dinosaur-size machine, like a tractor, with a huge, acorn-shaped four-leafed scoop on the front of it.

"What's that machine for?" I asked.

"That's what I usually use to move trees," the boss man explained. "It works pretty good in open country, but it's too big for yards like the one this morning. Besides," he added, "it takes a trailer to haul it."

I felt small. Lester and I were nothing more than substitutes for a hunk of steel. We had a job—and not a job anybody would want— maybe because of a machine's limitations, or if not, because our employer's trailer had a flat tire.

The boss man turned right, and a short distance later, he stopped. We were under the canopy of a grove of trees. Beyond the grove and a bit off to the right, the land opened. I could see waves of golden wheat, blue sky, and white clouds. It was like looking at a YouTube video of "America."

When it rained, the wheat field drained in our direction, muddying the little road on which we'd stopped, the boss man said. Tractors and pickups couldn't get into the field when that happened. It would be our job to dig a trench to divert the runoff. The boss man had purchased forty-five feet of six-inch black flexible plastic tubing; it lay on the ground a few yards in front of the pickup. The trench had to be about a foot deep, he said. We took our tools from the pickup and went toward the tubing.

The boss man said that he had an errand to attend to—probably lunch!—but that he'd be back soon.

The dirt where we were was dry, loose topsoil on the canopy's edge, nearest to the field. At its other end, under the canopy, it was covered with leaves and bits of rotting wood. I gave Lester the shovel for the softer end and took the pickax to the leafy end, which I knew would be crawling with roots.

Though most were no thicker than my thumb, the roots were stubborn and hard. Sometimes my blade bounced off them. Sometimes when I swung at them, I caught only an edge, and the root at which I was aiming merely flicked to one side, forcing me to swing again. With every three or four swings, I had to stop and catch my breath. My COPD was getting to me.

I sweated and panted and swung—it was above ninety degrees by now—and sweated and panted and swung, telling myself that if I got through the grove before the boss returned, he wouldn't notice the condition of my lungs. I kept my ears open for the rumble of his pickup.

Two or three times that morning, while digging the hole and unearthing the tree, I had heard a different sound, one that I presumed was a cell-phone ring. Soon I heard it again. But Lester didn't answer, and I didn't see any bulge in his pockets.

"Lester, what's that ringing I keep hearing?" I asked.

"Oh, oh," he said pleasantly. "That's my watch. I have a talking watch."

It was déjà vu, shades of my experience, forty years earlier, in the chemical plant.

Lester rolled up the sleeve on his blue cotton shirt, pointed to his left wrist, and showed me how his watch worked. It beeped on the hour and half-hour. He pushed a button, and a computer-style voice told him the time. The watch even had an alarm—he set it and rang it for me—that sounded like a crowing rooster.

Lester was smiling broadly. He liked his watch.

"I got it at Radio Shack for nineteen ninety-five," he told me, beaming.

We started to chat.

He explained to me that he had lost the sight in his right eye at the age of five when it had been hit—he didn't say how—by a "bunch of dirt." His vision had dimmed slowly over a couple of years, but ultimately, the eye went completely dead.

Cataracts came to his left eye when he was in his teens, leaving him with only partial sight in his "good" eye. When watching the television in the hall, he said, he saw only colors, not images. He said that the hardest thing for him at the labor hall was that "I can't see the line where I'm supposed to sign in."

He spoke in a kindly, cheery, boyish voice, frequently chuckling, all of it a bit too loud.

I asked him how long he'd been working out of the hall. About two and a half years, off and on, he said. "It's a pretty good place," he added.

That's when I began to wonder if Lester, in addition to being blind, might also be retarded. No one else would have said that the labor hall was "pretty good," even if he believed it.

In the hall that morning, Lester had been asleep in a chair. I had been sitting next to him for an hour or more. From time to time he had stirred, even opened his eyes. I had noticed that one of them was a bit bloodshot, but hadn't paid much mind. I've seen guys who were dead to the world while sitting in the hall, usually because they've been up all night, drunk or on drugs.

"Why were you asleep this morning?" I asked him.

Lester explained that he lived in a shelter for the homeless—he said it was a pretty good place too—which every afternoon, by computer, issued each of its prospective lodgers a number. Those holding numbers 1 through 200 got in for the night. Lester had drawn number 428.

"Then where did you sleep?" I asked.

"Oh, outside the shelter. They let us sleep on the grass there," he said, totally content.

But, of course, he hadn't slept well.

I asked Lester if, being blind, he wasn't eligible for a disability check of some kind. He told me that he received about eight hundred dollars a month—a little more, a little less, depending on how much he earned from working. But he had to pay fifty-three dollars a month for a storage locker where he kept some furniture for his mother, he said.

I couldn't figure out where the rest of his money might go, and that convinced me that my earlier suspicion had been right: Lester probably was a little retarded. In homeless shelters, good-hearted but slow-minded types acquire "friends" toward the end of every month— shortly before their checks arrive. On check day, and for two or three days afterward, they make loans to these friends. Of course, their friends then disappear, a feat that's especially easy when one's creditor is a blind man.

We went back to working, me picking and panting through the roots again. Before long, maybe an hour and a half after he'd left, the boss man returned in his pickup.

He stood and watched as I swung the pick—taking my time, so as not to set off panting. Lester scooped and dug. The boss man walked up and down the trench, pointing out spots for us to widen or deepen. When we had dug the distance that he had prescribed, we laid the tubing into the trench.

It was shallow by an inch or two.

The boss man looked worried. He sat down on a fallen tree trunk, trying to figure out what to do.

I told him that he should have bought four-inch tubing.

He didn't make any comment, but he did look at his watch. By then, it was nearly three o'clock. He had contracted our labor for seven hours, and had promised to meet our ride—a guy from the labor hall—at a service station at three thirty. He had us mount into the cab and drove us to the station, where he "signed," or filled out, our ticket—the half-sheet of paper that authorizes payment. He handed it to me. I glanced at the document with the usual concern in mind.

Not all employers behave alike, especially those who have bosses themselves. If, for example, a day laborer works eight hours under the supervision of someone who has a boss—an employee of a regional or national corporation, for example—the supervising employee, if he or she is empathetic or generous, will record nine or ten hours instead. It's a way to tip laborers with corporate fat. When a ticket is signed, day laborers look to see if hours have been added to the bill.

Our ticket credited each of us with only seven hours. I wasn't surprised—mom-and-pop operators are stingy sorts—but I wasn't pleased.

The afternoon shift at the labor hall was manned by two white males that day, Bruce, a red-faced and scornful middle-aged man whom the workers nicknamed Rush Limbaugh, and Jason, an officious but well-liked thirty-year-old. I gave our ticket to Jason. Scrutinizing it, he found a flaw.

"Look at this," he said, with the glee of a boy who has spotted an ugly bug. "The guy wrote down seven hours for each of you, but down here"—he moved a finger to the bottom line on the form—"where he's supposed to write in the total number of hours, he put 'seven' again."

"So what?" I said.

"He was supposed to put 'fourteen.'"

"Yeah, but look at the hours," I argued. "He listed them as eight thirty to three thirty and the ticket has both our names."

"But we bill him according to the total number of hours," Jason spat.

He said that he would telephone the boss man to get permission to change the notation on the ticket.

I was peeved: Filling out the ticket wasn't my job, I figured. If the boss man made an error, it was his problem, not mine.

Jason made the call but a recording machine answered. Lester and I waited. Jason called again. We waited again, fifteen minutes or more.

"What happens if the guy never calls back?" I blustered.

"Rush Limbaugh," seated behind the counter that divides labor-hall personnel from their charges, had been listening to our exchanges.

"If he doesn't call back, then we pay each of you for three and one-half hours," he said with finality.

That was enough for me. I walked out.

Ninety minutes later, when I came back, calmer but not having forgiven anyone, Lester was gone, the boss man had returned the call, and Jason had a check ready for me, pay for seven hours.

The check showed that the boss man had contracted us at $6.35 an hour, about 20 cents an hour above the minimum wage at the time. Our take-home pay for the tree-moving and ditch-digging was $40 and pennies, but that was before we paid $5 each for our ride.

I thought of the suburban teenagers who no longer do heavy-duty yard chores, and for the first time in my life, I envied them their leisure, their allowances, even their zits.

3

The Plant

The plant had been built in the late fifties or early sixties. Though it was not a facility on the scale of General Motors or Stalin's Five Year Plan factories, its buildings nevertheless dwarfed those who labored there.

It belonged to a privately held national company with four divisions, nine regional offices, and a factory in every state. It produced culverts, huge steel tubes or (according to a dictionary) "arched drains," plus gratings of various sizes and shapes. It sold its culverts to road and bridge crews.

The plant's buildings were of steel and fiberglass sheeting. Over the years, the outdoor sides of the steel sheets had acquired a patina of rust. Parts of the inside surfaces were rusty too, but their condition was harder to discern, because indoors—at least in the industrial work areas—the lighting was dim and the air full of smoke. The place smelled of burning metal.

Two buildings were on the plant's grounds. One was a low-roofed affair about thirty yards long, housing a break or lunch room, two industrial washrooms, and three or four administrative offices.

The plant's sparking, clanking work was performed in a structure far greater in size, nearly a hundred yards long, running east to west, with two arms, each about thirty yards long, that bracketed the low-roofed office-washroom building. This workshop building had a peaked steel, or "tin," roof and walls that stood four sheets of siding high, or, with allowances for overlap, about twenty-five feet tall.

Counting from the ground up, the third level of sheeting was of transparent fiberglass, a necessity since illuminating the cavernous interior would have been costly, even with neon-tube lights. But time and sunlight had clouded the fiberglass. The production workers labored in half-darkness because most of the light that reached them came from the north end of the wings, whose steel doors, thrown open, were wide enough for forklifts to enter carrying culverts fifty feet long.

The west wing of the gargantuan workshop held two long vats of steaming tar, into which, according to specifications from the buyers, some culverts were dipped for waterproofing.

The spine or central section of the place—the hundred-yard section that connected the east and west wings—was used for the storage of old equipment and new materials, mostly rolls of sheet steel from which the culverts were pressed.

Most of the work was done in the east wing. In its southern corner, beside a ten-foot doorway from which a little bit of light entered, sat the plant's principal piece of equipment, a blue, L-shaped machine—I nicknamed it the Hellmore, making fun of its brand name.

The machine's spine ran in a north-south direction, spanning nearly twenty feet. Its skeleton was of nine-inch-square steel beams, spaced about four feet apart. Lines supplying the machine with electricity, water, and compressed air snaked through its square tubing, curled around its body, and crawled beneath it on the concrete floor.

When he began to produce an order, the Hellmore's operator, using an overhead crane, brought a roll of steel, about six feet tall and four feet in diameter, to its rear, and with an assistant, mounted it on a huge metal spool—like loading toilet paper into its holder. Then, working on opposite sides of the machine, the two would pull the roll's free end down the spine, passing through two sets of rollers. In between the rollers were blank spaces, each about a foot long. When the machine was running, jets sprayed water into the blank spaces, keeping the process cool. The rollers pressed creases along the length of the steel, giving it a corrugated or ruffled form.

At the end of the rollers was an open space of about five feet, and at the crux of the L, a machine to curl the moving steel into the shape of a tube, like a peashooter made from a sheet of paper.

As the corrugated sheet twisted into a tube, creases aligned along its edges were pressed by another roller, crunching as they were crammed into place. Spiraling into shape, the culvert twisted past a huge circular saw as it moved eastward through a ten-foot opening, going outdoors. When the culvert reached the desired length, the Hellmore operator pushed a button to bring the saw's electric motor—as big as a kitchen range—into action against the still-spiraling tube. Sparks filled the tube's interior as the roaring saw cut. Barring breakdowns and glitches, it took an operator about half an hour to produce a culvert fifty feet long.

Most of the culverts weren't deemed finished once they were cut. The frame on which they rested, outdoors, stood above two sets of six sloping I-beams. When the Hellmore operator pulled a lever, the culverts fell onto the I-beams and rolled downward about twenty feet, toward a second monstrous piece of equipment called a re-roll machine. They came to a stop against vertical beams of steel, or sometimes, shoulder-to-shoulder against each other, forming a line.

The re-roll machine sat in a concrete-lined trench about six feet deep and sixty feet long, on steel tracks that ran east-west. Its operator, a gruff, red-faced man of fifty named Eduardo, worked from a cab at its eastern end. Attached to the cab's west side, facing the building, were three cone-shaped steel spools about two feet wide. An identical set of spools sat at the opposite end of the trench. Two boxy steel carriages, mounted on the same tracks as the cab, stood between the sets of spools. Thick electric cables connected them to each other and to the cab.

When Eduardo pressed a button, the vertical steel beams dipped and a culvert rolled onto the carriages, coming to rest with a boom. He then moved his cab along the track until its spools entered the culvert on both ends. With joystick controls like those used for video games, he positioned the spools against the inner edge of the culvert, then set it to spinning atop the carriages. The spools flattened the creases so that, for about eight inches from its end, the culvert's minimum diameter was seventy-eight, not seventy-seven, inches. The purpose of the rolling was to stretch the steel so that at its ends, one culvert could be slipped inside another. When culverts needed to be joined at both ends, Eduardo first spun the culvert against the spools at his end of the trench, then at the opposite, or western, end.

Once the re-rolling was completed, a matter of about ten minutes, Eduardo flipped a lever and steel arms lifted or kicked his culvert upward a few inches—high enough to clear the carriages and to drop onto a second set of six sloping I-beams, on which it rolled to a final brace of vertical bars or came to a stop against tubes that had already moved down the slope.

The I-beams stood about two feet aboveground. Among them— between them and atop them—is where I was put to work, always with a second man from the labor hall. Our chief task was painting the ends of the culverts to retard rust.

For us, the job began at seven in the morning, an hour after the regular employees punched a time clock in the break room. Our first task was mixing the paint, whose ingredients we brought from the building's long and dark central section. With an electric stirring device, we combined five-gallon cans of a gray, oil-based paint with five-gallon buckets of zinc dust; the result was a galvanizing, or rust-retardant, sludge. Then we'd go outside, roll the culverts apart, stabilize them with wooden chocks, and with four-inch brushes, daub our mixture onto their ends.

Painting wasn't hard, but it made a mess of our Labor-4-U hard hats and of our shoes, permanently splotched in gray after our first hour on the job. More troublesome, paint dripped onto our hands and faces, especially when we were working inside a culvert, reaching overhead. The plant's remedy—this was novel to me—was the popular lubricant WD-40. It didn't stink or irritate the skin like paint thinner does.

After we painted, forklift drivers hauled the culverts away, sometimes to the plant's ten-acre storage yard, where they were loaded onto trucks, or into the tarring room of the west wing, or to the east wing, where welders modified them, adding tabs and braces and sometimes smaller lengths of culvert, forming L's and T's.

This process, as I have described it, is only as accurate as textbooks are. In real life, at least during my days at the plant, production was a stop-and-go affair. When a new order was started, new rolls of steel, wider or narrower, or of a thicker or thinner gauge, had to be loaded and threaded, and rollers had to be reset. When a roll was almost consumed and a new one was brought, a workman had to unite the rolls with a weld.

Sometimes the rollers on the curler strayed a tad off their settings. When that happened, the machine had to be stopped and adjusted. Every now and then the steel sheeting came with a tear, or tore when passing through the rollers, and everything had to be halted so that it could be trimmed with shears or welded into one piece again.

Outdoors, unstretched culverts sometimes fell from the I-beams with too much force, knocking the carriages off their track; we had to descend into the trench, and with tall crowbars and brute force, right them. When drizzle was falling, we painters had to apply two or three times more sludge to get it to stick. When it didn't rain, our gloves slowly dried and the handles of our paintbrushes stuck to them. We had to chase up new gloves and dispose of the old ones.

Generally speaking, it took about twenty minutes to paint the ends of a culvert that had twisted and rolled for forty-five minutes to reach us. This meant that on our first day, we spent a great deal of time merely waiting, sitting on the I-beams.

Our introductory day, I suppose, was intended, like other rituals, to entice our return. The day had begun, to my surprise, with a parade of workers, including the foreman, bearing gloves, earplugs, plastic goggles, even smocks—safety-equipment gifts to show that the company cared.

But every day after that, when the production line wasn't moving, we were in motion, performing chores that would have fallen to others in unionized plants.

The most time-consuming of our idle-time tasks was cleaning the area around the Hellmore machine. The spray from its jets trickled onto the surrounding floor, forming brown, oily puddles two inches deep. Strewn across the floor were metal shavings, steel bands, and lengths of the kraft paper in which the rolls had been wrapped. Once we had removed the litter, we push-broomed the water outdoors. Then we pumped a degreasing detergent from a fifty-five-gallon drum into three-gallon garden sprayers and pumped the degreaser onto the floor and the machine. After that, we hosed the floor and machine, creating café-au-lait puddles that we swept outdoors.

Our assignment to chores that, in a union shop, would have fallen into a job category other than "painter" very nearly had a consequence that I could not have anticipated. The machine operators and welders, who often had to manipulate scraps of curled steel, wore boots with steel toes that were covered by an extra flap of thick leather, an "external metatarsal guard." Their boots, they told us, cost more than two hundred dollars, and their purchase was subsidized by the company. Most day laborers wear jogging shoes or, like me, simple brogans. As painters at the plant, we were not told to wear anything else. But when we were put on cleanup detail, we had to carry away curls of steel that had been cast aside during stoppages and repairs to the Hellmore machine. Some of the curls were six feet long and weighty. On my first assignment to cleanup duties, I lifted one of these, but with one of my gloved hands, lost my grip. The curl fell to the ground, striking one of my feet with such force that I could not walk for nearly ten minutes.

Welders kept their rigs in an area north of the Hellmore machine. Besides combining culverts to make T- and L-shaped products, they built grates of 1/4- and 3/8-inch plate steel and 3/8- and 1/2-inch rebar. Every weld on the culverts had to be painted, and when the welds were hot, our paint sizzled and our brushes smoked. The grates had to be painted, too, but with a different, store-brand sludge, ready-made in one-gallon cans. In the shop's dimly lit exterior, it was hard to distinguish between the gray of their rebar and that of our paint.

Despite stops and starts and mishaps like mine, the plant produced two dozen culverts a day, with a sparse staff: a superintendent, two office workers, a foreman, three forklift drivers, three welders, and two machine operators—a dozen in all, plus two painters, always Labor-4-U workers like me.

The legal and macroeconomic underpinnings of agency day labor have been thoroughly probed by a handful of academics, among them Professor Nik Theodore of the University of Illinois at Chicago, who, often in collaboration with others, has authored a dozen papers on the topic. In a 2007 contribution to a British economics journal about the American temporary staffing industry, or TSI, Theodore and a Canadian collaborator, Jamie Peck, outline the basics: "Temporary staffing agencies derive their income from fees charged to employers for the temporary employment of workers registered with the agency. Temps are paid directly by the agencies, which in legal terms are the 'employer of record.'"

Though contracts between agencies and their clients, or user firms, vary and their figures aren't disclosed to day laborers, both scholars guess that agencies charge client firms from 30 to 50 percent more than the agencies pay their workers. Those with whom I worked, however, said that our agency charged double the amount that it paid to us. At the culvert plant, we were paid $6.50 an hour, half of $13, the figure that the plant's employees said had been their starting pay.

The advantages that we, as temporary workers, provided are well known to sociologists. Theodore and Peck note:

Working through staffing companies, businesses are able to capture the benefits of *de facto* employment . . . while shedding many of the costs, risks and longer-term responsibilities that accompany *de jure* employer status, all courtesy of the agencies' employer-of-record designation. By insinuating themselves between the worksite employer and the employee, staffing companies shield firms from regulatory costs, such as exposure to unemployment insurance or workers' compensation claims, while also decoupling temporary workers from workplace benefits, such as health insurance and pensions entitlement.

Since corporations usually provide vacations, sick leave, and retirement benefits to their employees, even at thirteen dollars an hour Labor-4-U workers were a bargain for the culvert plant. The only fly in the ointment, from the point of view of our superiors anyway, was that we were laborers of a low-quality sort.

While scholars understand that agency day laborers are not privileged employees, I have not seen any detailed exposition of the internal dynamics of day-labor agencies in the pages of academic journals, apparently because academics don't take jobs as workers. What they have not spelled out is the means by which agencies rate their workers, and by which workers rank themselves.

But they get near. Theodore and Peck note:

> In what Gottfried (1992) aptly terms the "triangulated" employment relationship of agency-mediated work, the sociopolitical relations of the workplace are reconstituted: Temps are typically denied meaningful access to employment benefits; they tend to have lower wages and fewer prospects for career advancement than permanent workers; they are often alienated from both labour unions and co-workers; they are subjected to perfunctory workplace discipline, with little or no means of recourse; and they exist in a world of normalised insecurity.

Like all Americans, day laborers are stratified according to the venerable rule "Them that has is them that gets." Few day-labor agencies provide transportation to all of their workers; doing so would be expensive and would expose them to liability for traffic mishaps. Instead, most expect workers to get themselves to work. The first dividing line is between workers who have their own transportation and those who don't. Not only do drivers "catch out," or get dispatched, more often, but if they carry others to a job, they collect a fee—usually five to seven dollars—from each of their riders.

Day laborers are also divided into strata formed by their availability as part-timers or—the elite of labor halls—weekly-ticket types, men and women who are full-time day laborers assigned to jobs with distant ending dates. By arrangement with the client company and the labor hall, most weekly-ticket workers report to the work site, not to the labor hall. This arrangement saves the workers about two hours daily of unpaid waiting time. In return, they agree to take their wages, not daily, but one afternoon a week at the labor hall. Weekly-ticket work-ers are the favorites of labor-hall bosses because they put an agency's income on a nearly automatic footing.

Part-timers have ordinary jobs elsewhere. They come to labor halls only for what they call beer or gasoline money. But because schedules at their anchor jobs take priority, and because working more than sixty hours a week is a challenge to anyone, they often can't "repeat," or con-tinue on a day-labor job, day after day. Sometimes they cannot work a full day, and therefore are often picked for tickets that call for a mere four or five hours of labor.

Though outranked by weekly-ticket workers, part-timers are val-ued not only because they come with wheels but also because they have inured themselves to labor discipline. Few are felons, alcoholics, or ad-dicts, and they are unfailingly pliant and polite.

Weekly-ticket workers and part-timers make up perhaps 20 to 40 percent of the workforce at any reputable hall, but in normal economic times, a different type of laborer accounts for the bulk: the car-less, hapless, witless, footloose, or lazy day laborer of lore. Perhaps a fifth of them reside in homeless shelters and halfway houses; the rest live with their mothers, girlfriends, sisters, or wives. Day-labor agencies arose both to protect and exploit these men and a few women like them. For better or worse, they are the "regulars" of labor halls.

I was dispatched to the culvert job in an old white sedan whose interior was littered with hamburger wrappers and driven by a long-standing part-timer whom the regulars had nicknamed the Hulk after the comic book character. He was a dark-brown forty-six-year-old who often wore his hair in dreadlocks. He was an inch or two shorter than six feet tall, and he told me that he weighed 325 pounds. Two evenings and three nights a week, he worked at a warehouse. Almost every morning, he was at the labor hall.

Dolly assigned him to the culvert plant, I believe, because she knew that he would do a satisfactory job, and she was right: His brawn came in handy when we had to lift carriages back onto their tracks. He was quiet-spoken when he said anything, but he didn't chat much, a veri-table strong and silent type.

On our second day at the culvert plant he had to take off at three thirty, an hour before our usual time, to report to his regular job. I repeated the next day, but Hulk didn't show at the labor hall; perhaps his steady job had run into overtime. Dolly replaced him with a new face, part-timer Rob Thomas, who had recently been laid off from what he'd thought was a career.

Rob was in his early thirties, handsome and chocolate brown. He carried himself with his chin tilted slightly upward, as if he were staring at a ten o'clock sun. He said that he had spent a year or two in college and he spoke like a man who was no stranger to classroom discussion. He drove a spanking new full-size pickup with leather seats and, I assumed, had hefty installment payments to match.

Though he admitted that he had worked at Labor-4-U some years before, he had afterward married a nurse and gone to work on the second shift at a cinder-block factory, even taken out a mortgage on an exurban home. He'd worked at the cinder-block plant for three years, and his tax return for the previous year, he claimed—quite plausibly— showed $52,000 in income, a good deal of it from overtime: The plant worked a fifty-five-hour week.

A couple of months before, he said, he and his coworkers noted an anomaly in the plant's storage yard.

"We had blocks lined up all over the place. From that, we knew something was happening, we knew that business was slowing down. But they'd never had a layoff at the plant. They'd always put people to picking up trash, or doing something else," he told me.

The collapse of the building industry brought a new order of things. Two weeks after the workers had noted the stacks of blocks accumulating high and wide, the second shift was laid off. Rob was out of work.

He was eligible for $420 a week in benefits, he said, and the state's insurance program allowed him to earn $100 a week without penalty. He had come to Labor-4-U to earn that hundred dollars, about two days' wages. If he earned more than that, he warned me, "I'll be working for the government."

An ordinary shift for day laborers at the culvert plant ran nine hours, 7:00 a.m. until 4:30 p.m., half an hour being for lunch. Our gross earnings were about $57 a day, our take-home pay closer to $50. On our second day, Rob turned fretful because after six hours, he calculated, he would be "working for the government." When he asked that we be allowed to end the day early, the foreman was taken aback.

Our foreman, Fred, was a muscled and towering black man in his early forties who, to use a bygone term, was a scissorbill—a worker without class consciousness. At lunch on the breezeway outside the break room he told us that he sold Rolex watches at weekend flea markets. He bought them cheaply in lots of ten through obscure connections to a factory in Switzerland, he claimed, and he sold them for a thousand dollars each. The business didn't profit him much, he admitted, but he pursued it for tax deductions: He charged off his pickup, its gasoline, even his boots. A "high-powered accountant" worked wonders for him, he boasted.

He also declared that his hero was Donald Trump, the New York real estate billionaire. From Trump's writings and television talks, Fred said, he had learned the importance of risk. "If you hold on to money, it won't make you any money," he lectured us.

Though he said that he'd been at the culvert plant for twenty-one years, he professed to believe that he'd be rich someday. To top off his lecture, he offered to give us instructions that would lead us to golden destinies of our own. Rob and I, suspecting that he was winding up a pitch whose aim was to get us to invest a penny or two, merely nodded. We didn't believe a word he said.

Fred was annoyed when Rob asked for a shortened day, I believe, because reports from the other workers had told him that we were industrious guys—good candidates for a weekly ticket, at least. The plant had three openings for permanent, full-time workers, he claimed.

Rob's interest piqued, though he didn't believe that the starting wage would be as high as thirteen dollars—and Fred hadn't cited a figure.

As it turned out, Rob's hopes didn't matter anyway.

The plant, Fred continued, hired all of its workers as weekly-ticket men, converting them to permanent status after ninety days. To have a chance at a permanent job, it seemed, Rob would have to trust Fred—and to sacrifice his unemployment check.

I told Fred that I was sixty-two and was receiving retirement checks from Social Security. Labor-4-U, I said, was for me only a way of earning "walking-around money."

Rob didn't mention his unemployment check, but promised that he'd sign an application the following day if Fred let us leave early. Fred relented and Rob kept his word. But weeks later, when I ran into him at the labor hall, he said that the plant had never called him.

While Rob laid out, sticking to the $100-a-week limit, I continued at the culvert plant with a third partner for a couple of days. He said he needed to earn bus fare for a day in court—as a defendant—on assault charges in a trial set for a distant locale. On my last Friday at the plant, I was working with a regular, James Ling.

He was in his forties, about as brown as hardwood flooring, with a scar across his cheek and a balding, shaved head. Of unremarkable height and build, he usually wore short pants during summer months, and he always spoke, or barked, in what the military calls "a command voice." But he had a speech impediment. Nobody could readily make out all of his words, and though without complaint he would repeat what he'd said, he never spoke slowly enough to be fully understood. One of the old-timers at the hall whispered that Jimmy's problem was that he was under medication for a psychotic condition. "When he doesn't take his medicine, he talks even faster and works like a slave," the old-timer said.

The regulars sometimes mimicked Jimmy's speech, but nobody disliked him, in part because when he wasn't barking, his demeanor was humble and sincere. When others spoke, he listened with his head hung down, as if in sympathy or deep contemplation. When, in the usual labor-hall chitchat, he asked questions about work assignments and pay, it was apparent that he needed a job.

Jimmy was a car-less married man. His wife, he confessed—though he didn't have to confess, because nobody can support a spouse or children on labor-hall income—earned more money than he. If he had a criminal record, or ever drank or used cocaine, nobody noted as much. Everyone at the hall who knew Jimmy knew him to be a reliable working guy.

But bosses of various grades don't always see things the same way. On our first afternoon at the plant, while we were preparing grates, a half-dozen culverts stacked up outside and red-faced Eduardo called us away to paint them. After a few minutes, I noticed that while Jim's painting was careful and neat—mine never was—he was unusually slow. I finished two ends of a culvert before he finished the inside of one. Aware that he was falling behind, he changed the procedures for the job. Rather than standing on an I-beam to paint the exteriors, he brought an A-frame ladder from inside the east wing. It didn't improve his speed.

I said nothing, but Eduardo had his eyes on us.

The plant's three welders and two machine operators, including Eduardo—the men with whom we usually worked—were Central American immigrants, each with a decade or more in the United States. They were also men who didn't disown their heritage. They spoke to each other in Spanish even when nonspeakers were around, and during afternoon breaks, they insisted that the lunchroom's television be tuned to a Univision soap opera. At morning break, to please the plant's three blue-collar whites, or as Texans term them, Anglos—native English-speaking whites, with no Hispanic ancestry—the TV was tuned to *The Jerry Springer Show*.

I have been bilingual in Spanish since the age of fourteen, and for twenty-five years have been married to an immigrant from South America. Spanish is more than a second language to me; it has become a part of the way I think. Whenever I spoke to the Central Americans, I spoke in their tongue.

That had made me a novelty and a favorite of theirs. They encouraged me to apply for a permanent job, and asked me about my past and my private life. When the plant ran out of WD-40, they dug up hidden spray bottles for me. At noon, they offered me delicacies from their lunch boxes. When I arrived in the mornings, other workers merely nodded hello. The Central Americans gave me thumbs-up signs.

They also gave me a nickname, Abuelito, or "Little Grandfather," which I translated as "Pops." My Labor-4-U comrades carried it to the hall and the nickname stuck.

Overt hostility between racial and ethnic groups is now rare in blue-collar workplaces. Suspicions and prejudices are still voiced every day, but not across ethnic divides. Each segment of the workforce is openly cordial, if secretly wary of the others. But with me, Eduardo soon crossed the line.

After Jimmy and I finished the rush of culverts, Eduardo put Jimmy to push-brooming the storage areas of the plant. He told me to wash the area around the Hellmore machine. While I was doing that, he sidled up to me.

"Your buddy there is lazy," he declared.

"Why do you say that?" I asked.

"You saw him painting, same as me," he insisted. "He is slow, lazy."

"Well," I countered, "it's his first day. Maybe he just has to figure it out."

"No, they're all like that. *Los negros* don't want to work," Eduardo countered. "Even Fred is lazy," he added.

He did not use any of the common Spanish racial epithets, but he continued in the same vein. He said that years ago the plant had a staff of twenty African Americans. Today, he maintained, a smaller crew did the same amount of work; Fred was the only black in the plant. Eduardo added that the Hellmore operator, one of the Central Americans, had asked that I be given the job of cleaning around his machine because Hulk, the operator claimed, had done it in a perfunctory way.

Arguing with him was not appropriate to my station or standing at the plant, and it was clear that he wouldn't be persuaded anyway.

About four, Fred, the foreman, asked Jimmy and me to work until five thirty. We had come to the plant in the Labor-4-U van that morning with the understanding that it would pick us up at four thirty. We explained that we could ask its driver to come later, but couldn't promise that he would.

Fred was in a good mood. He volunteered to drive us to the labor hall, and to leave at five thirty on the dot, the hour when the plant closed, and he kept his word. On the drive to the hall in his super-cab pickup, he resumed his rap about how he needed to hire three men on weekly tickets, but to win an arrangement like that, he said, we had to be willing to work on the same schedule as the permanent employees at the plant.

"Pops here," he said, addressing Jimmy, "may use the excuse that he's on Social Security, but that doesn't go for you."

A weekly ticket was still open to me if I wanted, I suppose, but I had decided not to return in part because of Eduardo's speech about blacks, and in part because the plant's work schedule, even for day laborers, was wearying me.

At the culvert plant, we Labor-4-U men usually worked a nine- or nine-and-a-half-hour day, time enough. The plant's regular employees were—to use another antiquated term—wage slaves. They labored from 6:00 a.m. until 5:30 p.m., five days a week. They usually worked an additional six hours on Saturday, as Fred now wanted us to do, and sometimes they put in another six hours on Sundays.

"There ain't no way I'm working on weekends," I told Fred.

But Jimmy promised to report on Saturday, and Fred began quizzing him about his worthiness for weekly-ticket standing.

"You don't have a car? Then, do you know somebody who can bring you? Back when I was first starting here, I didn't have a car either, but I was determined to 'get on.' I hired people to bring me and pick me up. And I didn't pay them five or six dollars, you know, I paid them ten! I wanted to be sure that they'd be on time. You've got to be determined, man! You've got to want that job, you've got to want to work!"

His was a pep talk from a football coach, I suppose.

Jimmy didn't say anything, because he knew that to count on a driver, he'd probably have to pay ten dollars a trip, not ten dollars a day, as Fred had done years before. Fred probably knew as much too.

"If you haven't got a car, and you can't get a ride, well, have you got a bicycle? Can you get a bicycle?" he prodded.

Jimmy said that he would try, and Fred left us in proletarian peace at the labor hall.

On Saturday afternoon I was passing through the neighborhood when I saw an adult male in short pants riding a child-size bicycle down the street. From that day forward, for more than a month, Jimmy came to the labor hall on his undersized bike.

One morning, while waiting to be paired with another worker, he asked me to return with him. The company had bought blue cloth coveralls for its painters, he told me, trying to overcome one of my gripes about the place. His appeal was as if to a father or mentor. "You taught me that job," he said.

Despite his devotion to the culvert plant, nobody promoted Jimmy to weekly-ticket standing. In the end, and for reasons that he didn't explain, like the rest of us, he was waiting in the hall for a new ticket, any ticket, that would give him a day's wage.

4

THE SQUARE PEG

The hall where I reported for work was one of those one-story, flat-roofed, red-brick affairs built circa 1959 by what must have been called the Small Business Administration School of Ranch Style Architecture. In its era the building's clean and efficient lines—nothing wasted, not an extra penny spent—made it "modern." By 2007, when I first passed through its double glass doors, it was simply ugly and old.

It was also out of place. It sat about four blocks west of downtown in what, fifty years before, had been a neighborhood of African American manual workers. Though a small-scale housing project remained—the source of many of the hall's workers—the neighborhood had been gentrified over the decades. Most of the neighborhood's residents, by 2007, were college students and white-collar workers.

The building fit into its surroundings, or didn't, depending upon the hour. At five in the morning, it looked like any office building in any residential neighborhood, as if it housed an insurance agency or an optometry clinic. But by six, hard-bitten laborers were filing through its doors or loitering on its porch and driveway. At seven, the demographic began to shift, as joggers huffed past in nylon gym suits, young white men and women for whom physical activity was a pleasure, not a curse. By nine, when most laborers who didn't "catch out" had gone home, students were on its sidewalks. Their backpacks carried CDs and books, not work gloves and breakfast biscuits.

Inside the building was one big room, about fifteen feet by thirty feet, with offices and a restroom in smaller enclosures on its southern side. A dozen, sometimes two dozen, men and a clutch of women sat scattered among thirty-six plastic lawn chairs. Sometimes a dozen more stood around the room, and usually, a half-dozen people were outside, smoking. All the while a television set at low volume displayed images from newscasts and quiz shows punctuated by commercials from personal injury lawyers and payday lenders.

At the west end of the room stood a counter twelve feet long and nearly five feet tall, built of four-by-eight Masonite sheets, painted blue and topped with mock-mahogany Formica. When I entered each day, like everyone else, I went to the counter and signed my name on a list, putting an *N*, for "no," in a blank to indicate that I didn't have my own means of transportation.

On a swivel stool behind the counter sat Dolly, waiting for her telephone to ring. Sometimes it did ring. When it did, we could hear only mumbling. But afterward, if we were lucky, we'd hear a printer buzz as it printed a ticket.

One morning as I was waiting, a college-age man came in, a new face in the hall. He was tall, but his flesh was soft and his skin, very white. Auburn hair hung down to his shoulders. He wore a pastel T-shirt, cargo pants, and jogging shoes, plus a necklace on which hung a crystal and a five-pointed star.

Effervescent, he was talking to Stella, the office manager—a slender, narrow-faced white woman in her thirties—so loudly that the whole hall could hear.

"Most of my skills are office skills," he proclaimed. "I know Word and Excel and with a little brushing up, I could do PowerPoint as well. On my last internship in high school, I was classified as an assistant file clerk at an insurance agency."

The guy was obviously in the wrong place, a square peg in a round hole, I told myself. He should have gone to Kelly Services or Manpower, firms that specialize in temporary jobs for white-collar workers.

But he told Stella that he had a car and that, though they hadn't given him enough work, he'd signed on and briefly reported to two competing halls.

To weed out bad apples and paperless aliens, Labor-4-U, like a lot of temporary agencies, required applicants to show two forms of government-issued identification, and its filters sometimes caught people.

Most applicants cleared the bar by providing Social Security cards and driver's licenses—Mr. Office Skills had both—or Social Security cards and ID cards issued by the state to people who don't drive.

The agency also required prospective hires to pass a twenty-minute multiple-choice test.

The test I'd taken, which, from what I heard, was the same for everyone, included questions like these:

Which of the following drugs have you taken in the past week?
In the past year, how many times have you hit somebody?
If someone threatens you, how important do you think it is to fight to defend yourself?

A section of the test about workplace safety came with a ten-page booklet in whose text were embedded answers to all of its questions.

Office Skills had no trouble passing the tests and was soon briefly seated among the rest of us. As a newbie, he had an advantage. If an agency is short of workers, or if its dispatchers aren't satisfied with some of the regulars, they preferentially assign new recruits to tickets, churning the workforce to improve its quality, they'd say. From that first day and for the rest of the week, the agency kept Office Skills busy.

But when laborers fail to show for a repeat ticket, or turn down jobs, or simply can't handle the labor, dispatchers wordlessly put them on a second string, and Office Skills was benched pretty quickly, why I did not know. I had been put on the B-team myself, I believe, because I'd told Dolly that I didn't want to return to the culvert plant. Workers knew that business was unusually slow, or that they'd been benched, if they were still waiting for jobs when seven thirty came. Though some people hung around until nine or nine thirty, anybody who hadn't been dispatched by eight was probably facing a jobless day.

One morning about two weeks after Office Skills signed on, I found myself in the hall mainly with women, who—even though they tried their hardest and the hall's dispatchers did their best—were nearly always on the bench. Dispatchers were reluctant to assign them to tasks that were dirty or required prolonged exertion. The upshot was that when males were benched, they were placed in competition with women for jobs.

One of the regulars among the hall's laboring women was Little Carrie. Blue-eyed and in her late fifties, she couldn't have weighed more than ninety-five pounds. Perhaps because we were close in age, or because both of us were white, she often took a seat next to me.

She rented a room a block from the hall. I occasionally ran into her on my way to report, and on weekends, I'd sometimes come upon her walking a fluffy fifteen-pound white dog on a rope, not a leash.

Little Carrie was chinless, and on the street, it was obvious that she walked with a stiff gait, due to arthritis, she said.

Sometimes, she had told me, she house-sat for a lady on the other side of town. The house-sitting job was an after-hours affair; she had to be in the house at night but was free to leave during the day. When she was house-sitting, Carrie reported to an across-town labor hall, which usually assigned her to work in school and hospital cafeterias. Labor-4-U mainly sent her to office-cleaning jobs, and every now and then, to unloading trucks and opening and discarding boxes for retail stores.

Day labor for Carrie was a way to earn rent money, $250 a month, she said. She received $163 a month in food stamps, more than enough, she thought, and on Wednesday afternoons, if she wasn't at a day-labor job, she went to a nearby church to set tables for a fellowship supper, earning a meal and change. Twenty years earlier, before food stamps were issued via electronically readable plastic cards, she'd probably have sold her surplus to other workers in the hall. In those days, people also sold counterfeit bus-fare passes. But information technology has its drawbacks, and one of them, she told me, was that sometimes she still had food stamp credits when their expiration dates came.

That morning, while I was benched with Carrie, she reached into her purse, took out a tube of eyeliner and lipstick, even an eyebrow pencil, and tried to make herself "presentable." Chatting to a woman next to her, she said that she had a daughter who lived in Europe, but that the two of them were so estranged that she hadn't heard from her in five years.

Turning toward me, she said that she'd suffered from allergies the day before and had taken two tablets that had kept her awake until 4:00 a.m. During the brief time she'd slept, she dreamed that while wearing jeans, she'd found ten dollars in a front pocket.

"I was rubbing myself right here, where the pocket would be, when I woke up," she said.

B-teams at day-labor halls, I thought, are for people who dream about ten-dollar windfalls.

Sitting near us, as long as she could sit, and otherwise pacing in nervousness around the hall, was Gladys, a woman in her forties who was not much taller than Carrie but was of a much different kind. She wore rhinestone post earrings—Carrie had only a watch—and had a tattoo on each shoulder, though given her blackness, their designs were hard to discern.

Gladys's face reminded me of that of the late writer James Baldwin, but her hairdo was never unkempt—or un-thought-out—as his was. When she first appeared at the hall, her hair was in an Afro, perhaps an inch long. A month later, she practically skinned her head. After that, she adopted a Mohawk.

She had come to Labor-4-U from another hall, which, she complained, dispatched women only to restaurant and office jobs. Gladys wanted to earn a living just like the men—and even more, to work two tickets a day, one in the mornings, one at night. She claimed that she had been a long-haul trucker in an earlier stage of life, and also boasted that once, for a hall in Las Vegas, she had labored thirty-six hours non-stop. She said that she had come to Labor-4-U because she needed to earn a thousand dollars to pay for repair work on her car.

Her countenance was usually a frown. She spoke in a gruff voice, and despite the sign saying that workers should not crowd around the counter, Gladys was often there, pleading.

Desperation served her well. Within a week of her debut, she was strutting in steel-toe boots and a hard hat, not like the items the agency provided, but store-bought. The cost, I suppose, was negligible for her, since she paid no rent. On mornings when I arrived at the hall before five thirty, she was standing in its front yard, washing up at a hydrant. Gladys slept on a roll of blue foam, which she hid behind a bush on the eastern side of the hall.

It wasn't that she had anything against shelters, she said. The problem was that the city buses didn't start their routes early enough to allow her to be first on the sign-in sheet.

Within a couple of weeks of her first day, Gladys had developed a reputation at Labor-4-U. Dispatchers and managers liked her because she proved capable of handling any job, and the men only complained that she worked with too much brio, making them look lax.

Gladys was telling me about a ticket that she had gotten the night before when I heard Dolly call my name, followed by that of the Office Skills guy. It must have been about six thirty.

The job she had for us, Dolly said, was an eight-hour gig, "cleanup" at a construction site. Such jobs are common at day-labor halls, but their particulars varied widely. Sometimes construction cleanup was push-broom and mop work, indoors, dusty or muddy and dull, but hardly exhausting. Sometimes cleanup involved carrying scrap sheets of weighty plywood, short lengths of steel beam, or sacks of hardened cement, and that was a challenge for anyone.

Office Skills and I were assigned to a drugstore project in a suburb. We didn't know whether we'd be called upon to work indoors, outdoors, or both. He drove. His vehicle was a 2006 Buick in whose interior he'd tossed dozens of job application forms and empty bottles of springwater. As we rode, he played a CD whose music sounded to me like the chants of medieval monks. It was from a group called Nox Arcana, he said, telling me that the name came from Latin and meant something on the order of "Night Magic." He also told me that its creators saw themselves as providing a sound track for the stories of Edgar Allan Poe.

That he would mention Poe gave me a feeling of dread. Not

many men who know an author's name know how to tote plywood and cement.

Cleanup on construction jobs is customarily the responsibility not of subcontractors—carpentry, masonry, electrical, plumbing, roofing, or flooring crews—but of the GC, or general contractor, the person or firm with overall responsibility for a project. GCs never show up on time. Our ticket called for us to report at seven, but of course, no one was there but a crew of Mexican plasterers, already high in the air on scaffolds placed against the outside walls of the red-brick shell of the drugstore. Them, and a trucker from Texas.

We chatted with the trucker. He had come from a plant in Mississippi to deliver a half-dozen light poles, and like us, was waiting for the GC. In the cab of his 18-wheeler was his traveling companion, a shaggy dog named Floosie. Ours was one of three unloading stops that the pair would make before picking up cargo for their return on what would be a six-day trip, the trucker said.

Gasoline and diesel prices were climbing, and the trucker told us that on this run, he was averaging 7.4 miles to a gallon. With heavier loads, he said, he got as little as 6 mpg. Prices didn't bother him, he claimed, because his company paid for fuel, about $1,500 per tank. He made payments only on his $130,000 rig.

Perhaps because he sized up Office Skills the same as I did, he asked why the young man wasn't in college.

"Oh, I tried that," Office Skills said, "down where my parents live. But the college I went to had a cybercafe and I spent all of my time playing video games." He had come to Labor-4-U "mainly to get away from my folks," and was living in a rooming house whose landlady, a middle-aged woman, had thus far given him room and board in exchange for chores.

Our chat lasted an hour and maybe a bit longer. Finally, a half-dozen Anglo electricians arrived and told us that the GC's second-in-command was on-site, in the GC's trailer on a corner of the lot.

Office Skills and I reported—to a fortyish man whose appearance almost made me laugh. He was of average height and a bit thin, but with a wide black mustache that drooped to his chin. He wore short pants and had spindly legs. His torso was swallowed in a pearl-button western shirt, and on his head sat a safety helmet in the form of a cowboy hat. From the waist down, he looked like a scoutmaster, from the waist up, like the sidekick to a sheriff in a Wild West serial.

Our job was outdoors, he said. Between the building and the two busy streets that bordered it was asphalt-clad parking space, and on its three sides, a band of dirt about twenty feet wide that landscapers were to sod with grass. Both the parking area and the band of soil were littered with the detritus of construction work: sections of discarded plastic pipe and steel electrical conduit, foam and fiberglass insulation, broken bricks, and the thin steel posts that in some structures are used as substitutes for pine studs. The curbing was here and there covered with runoff dirt, and at places, tradesmen had piled waste materials against it. The foreman pointed us to a shovel, a spade, and a push broom, and we headed off to our task.

We had been scraping and sweeping the curbing for not more than twenty minutes when Office Skills said that he had to go to his car, where he had left a tube of sunscreen lotion.

Not more than half an hour later, he went back to apply it a second time.

Soon we were piling bricks in stacks that the GC's Bobcat—a gasoline-powered vehicle that's a cross between a forklift and a backhoe—would haul away. We were also carrying empty cement sacks and strands of steel wire to a Dumpster. From his seat on the Bobcat, the Cowboy Foreman was "rednecking" us, as black workers say, keeping us under his eye, pointing out overlooked or unseen tasks, giving orders, measuring our worth.

He put us to carrying lengths of rebar to a spot just below his trailer-office. Office Skills was straining; for every trip he made, I made one and a half. When we'd finished toting the rebar, the Cowboy pointed to a mound of king-size cinder blocks, also on the would-be lawn. They were heavy—to me they felt like forty pounds—and I could carry just one at a time. But Office Skills didn't know how to carry. He'd grab a block and hold it below his waist, practically straddling it while walking.

He knew he wasn't up to par.

"I'm a total couch potato," he huffed as we passed on the block-carry detail. "I'm a gamer. I'm not competent at physical work."

Since we'd not started until about eight thirty, morning break seemed to come early at ten. Office Skills disappeared into the shell of the building on his way to his car on the site's lawn-less side. He had to get something to eat, a snack he had prepared, he said.

I was leaning against the outside wall of a corner of the building, where a watercooler sat. The Cowboy came up to me.

"I'm going to send your buddy home," he blustered. "He's not working and I won't put up with that."

Cowboy didn't give me time to comment.

"I've had 'em like him before, and every time, I send them home! I ain't afraid to do it, no way!" he snarled.

He may have continued this tirade for a while longer, but finally I got a chance to speak.

"You've got to do what you've got to do," I said with the deference appropriate to addressing one's boss. "But he's just a kid. Maybe he'll learn."

I think the Cowboy was fazed that I didn't feel complimented. One of the saddest things about the construction business is that usually among bosses, and sometimes even among workers, a macho work ethic prevails. If a worker can't lift, shove, carry, push, or bang with enough force or speed, a real man will stick out his chest and fire the weakling on the spot: That's what the ethos requires. It's as if readiness to fire someone is a test of a supervisor's manliness.

Machismo of that sort is heartless in purely male settings, but its most common victims are jobless women. A few days earlier, Dolly had sent four women to a cleanup job, only to have the foreman refuse to let them enter the site. Dolly filed a complaint with government authorities, but that didn't give the women a job for the day.

If Office Skills was a burr under his saddle, I told the Cowboy—stretching the truth a bit—he was the same for me, because I had been carrying more and moving faster to make up for the kid's weakness or sloth. But I'm man enough to take it, I was trying to say.

The Cowboy sighed, as if taking pity on me—for defending the kid, not for my labor. Then he took a drag on his cigarette and turned his head, looking around, as if in thought.

He spoke again. "Who is driving, you or him?"

When I explained, he hurled his cigarette to the ground, snuffed it with a heavy shuffle of his foot, and, I swear, spat to the side.

I reminded him that even if we left, he'd have to pay us for four hours, the minimum charge at Labor-4-U.

"Well, look," he said, as if nearly ashamed. "You warn him that I'm about to send his ass out of here."

I nodded and he went away.

When Office Skills returned from his car, we fell in file to follow the Cowboy to the back of the structure. As soon as he was gone, I called Office Skills aside.

"Listen, the boss told me that he wants to fire you," I said.

The kid didn't comprehend.

"What for?" he asked.

"Because he says you haven't been working."

"But I've been working," he whined.

The trash on the building's back side wasn't as plentiful as elsewhere, and the Cowboy was off riding his Bobcat somewhere. I began to pick up lumber near a spot where a crew of three black masons was working. I carried the lumber a few feet and made a stack on the parking lot. Office Skills questioned our need to do that.

"Look," I told him, trying to teach him the ropes. "My job is moving stuff. I get paid for that. If I move stuff that I'm not supposed to move, they'll pay me for moving it back."

I was trying to tell him that we had to stay busy, whether our labor was useful or not. But he didn't understand. Instead, he walked over to the masons and asked which boards we needed to carry away. The result of the conversation was that I had to carry a half-dozen boards back to them.

I moved around the corner, still picking up trash, and Office Skills wandered off, for what purpose, I didn't know. When he returned, he asked me what time we'd break for lunch.

I told him, "Probably at noon."

He said that's what he figured, but that he'd asked the Cowboy, whose answer had been, "When I say so."

"Yeah, it's when he says so," I told him.

"But that's not fair," he said.

I guess the kid thought he was in high school, where customs are rules.

I told him that in English we have a word, "shamming," which means to look busy, pretending to work even when doing nothing useful. To make the point, I caught one of the Mexican plasterers as he was passing by, and asked for the equivalent in Spanish: *"hacerse buey,"* or "make like an ox." I explained to Office Skills that every worker knew, in one language or another, that shamming was a part of our jobs.

About noon the Cowboy reappeared, telling us that it was lunchtime. Office Skills and I crossed the street to a sandwich shop, where he ordered vegetarian fare.

As we ate, he told me that the day before, he'd worked on a crew whose job was tying wire around cross points in rebar, in preparation for a cement crew. During the course of our conversation, I learned that though he'd driven a crew of four others to the work site, he hadn't known that they were supposed to pay him a fare. Nobody had paid— and that meant, I was sure, that they despised the guy.

Perhaps twenty minutes after we returned to our chores, Office Skills told me that bending to pick up trash made him dizzy, and that "I can't work under the sun. It just drains my energy away."

"Why don't you tell that to Dolly the next time she gives you a job?" I asked, out of patience by then.

Fortunately, we were winding up the work at hand. Before two, we were done. The Cowboy had us stack our shovels and broom outside his trailer, then opened the door, sat down at a desk, and asked for the ticket, which I had in my shirt pocket. He filled it out and told us so long.

I glanced at what he'd written, five hours for Office Skills—an accurate figure—and seven for me. As an old hand on the day-labor range, the sheriff's deputy knew how to inflict a little pain.

Gladys, and even Little Carrie, I believe—and any of the women at the hall—could have done our job more ably than Office Skills, and Gladys, more ably than me. But I think it's unlikely that the Cowboy would have welcomed them, and even if he didn't send them home, he'd have probably called a competing agency when he next needed a crew.

A couple of weeks later, Office Skills drove up to the hall and asked a group of us who were standing outside where he might find another day-labor agency. He had been "terminated," he said, when he'd come in from a ticket the day before. "I guess I wasn't able to do the job," he said sheepishly.

"You should go to Manpower," I told him.

He said that he'd already applied.

Nobody else spoke to him.

He asked if any of us could loan him fifty dollars, which he claimed he needed by the end of the day "for rent." Maybe his landlady had soured on him, just as the dispatchers had.

Day laborers aren't heartless. Two-dollar and five-dollar loans are an everyday affair. But fifty dollars is money that can only fall from the skies.

Nobody took up a collection for Office Skills, and perhaps more telling than that, nobody informed him—and I did not recall it at the moment—that only blocks away a plasma collection center was paying new donors fifty dollars a pint.

5

A Real Deal Job

Dolly called for five men who didn't have cars, for a ticket "to un-load trucks." I leaped to the counter. Others crowded behind me. The job, Dolly said, was at a shopping mall within walking distance. That meant that we wouldn't have to pay a fare. It was the start of a perfect day.

Dolly gave the ticket to Jimmy, the tentative and reticent guy whom I knew from the culvert plant, and we followed him out of the hall. Holding the ticket made Jimmy's personality change, made him feel like he was in charge of our crew, I suppose. Walking at nearly a trot, he launched into a rant about how "when guys work for me, they better *work*!" The rest of us were, more than anything, amused that he took himself to be our boss.

"Speedball, you got to learn to slow down!" a guy named Tyke told him, invoking a nickname that I hadn't heard. "We're sup-posed to work, yeah, but not so fast as you! We supposed to do our work right, not rush around and get hurt! You got to learn to take it slow!"

Jimmy wasn't listening. He kept hectoring us in his rapid-fire speech about how we shouldn't slack, waving the ticket to punctuate his sermonette.

"You, you work as fast as you walk!" Tyke scolded.

Tyke was a fifty-seven-year-old who wore a nylon knee brace like mine. He was a short, thin man, no bigger than me, but with muscled forearms and biceps. He usually wore Starter athletic gear, jogging pants in winter, basketball shorts in summer, a New York Yankees cap on his head. His clothing always fit so well that it seemed painted onto his mahogany frame.

Every sentence that Tyke spoke, about anything whatsoever, ended with an exclamation point, and he wasn't shy about tooting his own horn either. He had recently moved from a house trailer to a new suburban condominium, he frequently bragged, and his wife didn't have to work because "she's got a nice little disability check," he said. "I'm hoping to get me a little disability check in a couple of years!" he usually added.

Tyke worked the night shift at a warehouse of a big-box store, but he came to the labor hall early every morning, willing to work even four-hour tickets, which, after taxes and fares, paid only pennies more than twenty dollars per day. He claimed to have ten grandchildren and three great-grandchildren, but in the time that I knew him, I never noticed him to show an interest in anything but money and impressing our bosses.

His exchange with Jimmy, I suppose, was aimed at challenging Jimmy's pretensions to leadership. But it was an exercise in hypocrisy. Tyke never took it easy, and everybody knew it. He was a dynamo at work, performing chores with the speed and spirit of a twenty-year-old.

The verbal sparks between Jimmy and Tyke had only started when we came upon a towering jet-black man in sunglasses, coming toward us on the sidewalk. His jaw, bristling with gray stubble, was bony and massive, dominating his face. He wore a long black leather coat, a black baseball cap on his head, and, as always, black jeans and black jogging shoes—size 15, he would later tell me. He waved as he neared us and his mouth opened in a broad, wordless smile that revealed widely spaced teeth.

Everybody knew the guy. He was the one who, had he been at the hall on time, would have led a crew to our job.

"Real Deal is back," somebody said.

A couple of guys high-fived him as we passed.

Real Deal was the central figure at the labor hall—when he was there, anyway. Everybody not only knew him, but had an opinion about him. His presence was so notable and so controversial that had I ever needed to verify that someone was a regular, I'd have simply said, "Oh, yeah? Then tell me a Real Deal story."

I had first heard of him two years before I set foot inside the labor hall. "He's the life of the party," The Hulk told me. On our first day at the culvert job, I'd asked The Hulk for his take. "Real Deal didn't use to be the way he is now. I think he fell off the boat somewhere," he said.

Tyke launched into a Real Deal anecdote as soon as we passed.

"The last time I worked a ticket with him, it was a mess!" he complained. "We were unloading at a furniture store! Customers were there! It was business hours, you know!"

Real Deal, he said, had been cursing a blue streak, not because he was infuriated, but because that was his usual way of speaking. A manager had heard him—Real Deal was practically shouting—and was peeved because he knew customers could hear too. He'd told Tyke to silence Deal.

Tyke recounted what he'd said:

"I told him, man, they can put us in jail for cussing! They'll do it too! Maybe you like going to jail, maybe some people get used to it, but not me, no sir! I ain't got no criminal record! None! Nothing! I don't want to be going to jail, so I keep my mouth shut, and you'd better do the same!"

Real Deal had gone quiet after that, Tyke claimed with a touch of pride.

Deal usually came into the hall relatively late, a few minutes after seven, because buses didn't run to his neighborhood early enough, he claimed, though most people suspected another motive: Most convenience stores, which sell beer, didn't open until 7:00 a.m.

The hall was usually packed when he made his entrance. Taking long, slow, stiff steps, he'd ease up to the counter, greeting his constitu-

ents like a senator passing through an airport. "Just the facts!" he'd
holler, though nobody knew why. "Yeah, just the facts!" his admirers
would respond. Then he'd put his signature on the sign-in sheet. "Real
Deal," he'd write. Only the dispatchers and a couple of cronies knew
his real name.

Deal always sat by the south wall of the waiting room, surrounded
by three or four minions. In raucous voices, they'd trade tales about the
booze they had consumed and the outrages they'd committed in the
foregoing days.

Real Deal spun the best of these stories.

"Sunday morning, it was about seven when I got there, and I told
that manager guy that if he didn't open up his store, I'd take my Labor-
4-U key and open it myself. I picked up a brick and pointed it at the
window and I told him, 'You really want to try me?'"

Everybody laughed when Deal told tales like that.

Sometimes a subordinate, feeling confident, would retell the legend
about a Saturday when Deal, lacking money, tried to hire a prostitute
with food stamps.

"Well, I figured that a whore who spends all day sucking dicks must
be hungry! I bet she was already on food stamps," he'd say.

On days when his mood was soaring, Deal talked about how he
wasn't a Labor-4-U worker but a "Later-4-U" man.

Deal and his corps often berated and sometimes refused offers when
they were called to the counter. "Shovel work? We ain't doing no *shovel
work!* No way, José," two or three of them would shout.

When the hall grew quiet and tickets were few, to break the monot-
ony—and, perhaps, the despair—of his peers, Deal would rise, raise his
arms above his head, and bellow, "Where's my truck? I'm the unloading man!"

Deal and his acolytes were firm in a preference for unloading work.
Sometimes they would wait until late in the morning, eight thirty or
nine, turning down other jobs on the chance that a call for an unloading ticket would come.

Six and a half feet tall, with broad hands that dropped as low as
his knees, Deal was unusually fit for furniture jobs. He could wrap his

long arms around a box of any size and pick up a chest of drawers from its base.

But that wasn't why he preferred moving jobs. Instead, it was because they usually ended in less than four hours and sometimes ended with a tip as well. Especially when female tenants hired laborers to move from one two-bedroom apartment to another, hours were short and tips were fat, twenty to thirty dollars. On moving jobs, one could earn the four-hour minimum in an hour or two, and with a tip, a full day's wage in half a day.

The dispatchers honored Real Deal's preference, even saved tickets for him, perhaps because he was practically a member of their family. He said that he'd been working out of the labor hall for eleven years, and nobody, including the hall's staff, had been around long enough to dispute the claim.

Deal had been a regular so long that he'd taken over one of the half-dozen chalkboards that lined the waiting room's walls. Everybody knew that the green chalkboard on the east wall was his. He used the board to record extemporaneous poems.

His last composition—predating the renown of Barack Obama—had been:

Change True but Real
Change to embrace the unknown
To collide with the unsuspecting truth
To realize that life has its ends, and change
True but real—to a heart.

Forget about the lies of the past,
Lies of the past, broken cobblestones.
Change the negativity, embrace life.
Change and live our dreams
At last live our dreams.
At last.

Within days of his return, on a whim he'd written a new poem on the board:

Breaking Through the Storm
Seeds of a depressed nation, life's abyss
Reality creeps through the nexus of sin
Tit-Tat, we cry out to the heavens for help,
Pain of endless chaos, prices rising
Give us a little help.

The problem with Real Deal, everybody knew, wasn't his persona or even his poetry. It was that he drank, and when he drank too much, he got rowdy.

Without telling anybody, I checked his police records, which showed that over the previous eleven years, his tenure at the hall, Real Deal had been charged with thirty-nine criminal offenses, usually in multiples, three to four times each year. Several of his run-ins involved charges of resisting arrest.

Typical among the reports was one describing an affray at a convenience store near the labor hall at seven thirty in the morning, apparently when Deal had slipped out of the hall on a beer run. A police report stated that he had approached the store's cash register with a beer and four adult magazines in hand. A dispute erupted and, the arresting officer asserted, Deal threw "various store items from the cashier counter" at the store's Pakistani attendant, who telephoned 911. Deal went outside in a fit of pique and before the police arrived, perhaps to show his displeasure with the attendant, "without authority forcibly broke into a coin-operated machine with the intent to steal property or money therein." The arresting officer booked Deal for assault and recommended that he be sentenced to a substance-abuse program.

On the morning that we passed him, he was returning to work after twenty-one days in jail, "for the usual, open bottle," he said. "I got three hots, no cot, just a mat on the floor," he told us.

Had Dolly known that he was on his way, she would probably have reserved our unloading job for Deal and his troupe, just to welcome him home.

After Tyke told his Real Deal story, somebody else complained about a turn at work with Deal. The speaker had been on a crew that had been sent back to the hall from a job, unpaid, a few weeks earlier because a foreman had found a fresh, if empty, can of 211—Deal's favorite, a potent beery brew—at the work site.

"The boss man sent us back, and you know, Dolly and everybody had to know whose 211 that was—it ain't no mystery, if you get what I mean—but nobody said nothing," he grumbled, though he, too, had apparently kept mum.

After passing Deal, the five of us reached the shopping center in minutes, at about seven, with half an hour to wait. We scattered onto bus-stop benches and a couple of us were lucky enough, or sleepy enough, to catch a catnap.

Our job was to prepare for the opening of a women's-wear outlet owned by a national chain store. Before long a middle-aged white man drove up in an SUV. He opened the location's door and called us inside. Its rectangular space was empty except for chromed clothing racks and a counter at the far end of its front, or retail, room, which had a floor of polished mock limestone. Between the retail room and a rear space that served as a storeroom were three or four fitting rooms carpeted in black. Two small bathrooms stood just inside the storeroom.

A cube truck—a short-bed truck with a box mounted behind its cab—pulled up outside. Its driver dismounted and opened the cube's door. Inside, he said, were 183 boxes. All of them bore the chain's logo and were of the same size, about twenty-four inches by eighteen inches by twelve inches. They were light. We carried them into the merchandise room and stacked them in three rows, each four boxes high.

About the time we finished, a middle-aged white man with a flat-top haircut appeared, a second boss. I followed him into the storeroom, in which a dozen tubular steel shelves sat. Remnants of construction materials—tiles, buckets of mastic, cans of paint—sat on a few of them. The new boss told me to move these items to the shelves in the rearmost part of the room. Among the remnants were ceramic flooring tiles.

I knew that tiles were troublesome. They are usually bundled ten or twelve together, or boxed, sometimes with as many as two dozen to a box. If the tiles are large, the packets and bundles are ponderous.

When they must be lifted from a position lower than your waist, they can cause lower back injuries.

I was careful moving them, observing the standard rule "Lift with your legs, not your back," that requires you rise from your haunches; don't bend over. It had always worked for me.

At the bottom of a stack was a bundle of 12 x 18 tiles, sheathed in Styrofoam. Because they sat on a shelf in a corner of the room, I didn't have enough space to maneuver so that I'd be squarely in front of the bundle: I had to pick it up one-sidedly, as if I'd spread my legs and were tying my right shoe. I took a breath, squatted, and lifted the stack. As I rose, my lower back winced. It only hurt for a minute.

The crew-cut boss man had come up to the storeroom's entry door— I suppose to see how my labors were progressing—and was apparently impressed with the speed with which I'd approached my chores.

Or else he'd taken a good look at the rest of the crew.

"We need one man to help us put merchandise onto the racks to-morrow," he said. "I want you to be here."

"What time?" I muttered.

But it didn't matter what he said. Though I didn't explain, I had already decided that I wasn't going to return alone because, being the only white on the crew, I wasn't sure that he hadn't picked me because of my race. I didn't want the other workers to see me as a beneficiary of prejudice, because I needed their goodwill more than I needed Flat Top's one-day job.

After I'd finished rearranging the storeroom, I joined the others outside on the bus-stop benches. Another truck was due, somebody said. Two guys went scurrying to a nearby vending machine to buy soft drinks. The rest of us reclined on the benches and fell asleep. Perhaps fifteen minutes later somebody shook me, saying, "The truck is here."

The new cube truck carried some 120 boxes on wooden pallets that had arrived by air freight, its driver told us. Some of the boxes were square and squat, some tall and thin. We unloaded them on the side-walk in front of an adjoining store, which hadn't opened yet. Then we began carrying the boxes inside.

A sticker bearing a number had been affixed to each box. We

formed a line leading up to Flat Top, every man with a box in his arms. As each of us reached the front of the line, he called out the number on his box. Flat Top stood by with a list of numbers, checking them off as we passed by. From the numbers, he knew what was in every box, and told us where to put them.

When we were at the back of the line, we made small talk with Flat Top and his partner. They told us that they did nothing but travel, opening stores for the chain in one town after another.

"I live in motels," Flat Top complained. "Sure, I have a house and pay a mortgage, but I'm never home."

When the new cube truck was empty, one of our bosses opened a box that contained office supplies, including three box cutters. He handed one to me. Those of us with blades opened the numbered boxes and cut away their tabs. Under direction from the boss men, two others put their contents into drawers in the counter and in a nearby desk, while the fifth of us flattened the boxes and carried them to a Dumpster. When we blade-wielders had opened all of the boxes, we helped distribute what they contained.

Some of the boxes were loaded with stacks of plastic and paper bags imprinted with the chain's logo, or bundles of tissue paper used for wrapping. In other boxes we found markers, pens, paper clips, and in others, wastepaper baskets. One box contained a file cabinet; another, a microwave oven; and a third, a small refrigerator—all brand-new. The clothing steamer that we found was no surprise, but I was stunned that the chain had air-freighted rolls of toilet tissue, soaps, and detergents for the bathrooms. A huge supermarket was located less than a block away.

"This is everything that a person could need," I said in amazement.

"Yes, we don't want these ladies to have to do anything but sell clothing," one of the bosses told me.

I was too timid to ask if, when stores ran out of toilet tissue, the central warehouse flew in replacement rolls.

We finished unloading the office supplies by 10:15 and went outside to the benches again. About ten thirty we were wondering if another truck would be coming when Flat Top came up, pulled the ticket from his pocket, and began making notations. He handed the ticket back to Jimmy, who turned toward us, fingers outstretched to signal "seven." We were overjoyed. Every man rose to his feet, skipped over to Flat Top, and shook his hand. Then we fell in together to return to the hall.

"They gave us seven hours because we're a good team," Jimmy boasted.

"Nobody, man, was just laying around! We got the job done!" Tyke said.

"Yeah, didn't nobody lay around!" someone else exclaimed.

Though I said nothing, I was a bit startled that my coworkers took pride in pleasing our bosses. Nobody mentioned Real Deal, but everyone had to know that our gain had been his loss, and that, now that he was back at the hall, it might be weeks before any of us landed a cushy job again.

An afternoon dispatcher was on early duty at the hall when we arrived. He took the ticket from Jimmy and noted that it called for two men to repeat. Looking at the group of us, he pointed out a pair—I was not included—and declared, "We want you back on that same job tomorrow morning." Apparently, when filling out the ticket, Flat Top had not specified which workers he wanted to return. I was relieved that I wasn't a racial standout.

For me, it had been a perfect day.

But the next morning, I could hardly pull myself out of bed. My lower back hurt. I didn't report to the hall. Not until late in the afternoon was I able to stand erect without pain. I paid a visit to a chiropractor, then drove to the nearest drugstore and bought a fifteen-dollar nylon back brace, which I thereafter wore beneath my shirt every day. I did not report the injury to Labor-4-U, because even when a day laborer gets hurt, unless he incurs a severe disability, his recovery time is his own misfortune.

6

Just for Fun

About eight thirty that morning three of us were chatting in the auction shed—me, a burly Automax mechanic, and a skinny used-car dealer who had a pencil-line mustache.

The shed was a wooden, peaked-roof structure, painted white, with a big door-less opening at its middle. It lay at the north end of an unpaved parking lot about a hundred yards deep. The lot, which was some two hundred yards south of a highway, was enclosed with chain-link, or "hurricane," fencing. Eighty to a hundred used cars sat on the lot in four rows that ran north and south.

Pacing, I had estimated the shed's western side, where we stood, at about twenty by twenty-four feet. A patch of unpaved ground about four yards wide lay between us and the eastern side of the shed, where the auctioneers held court. When Automax, the affiliate of a national used-car chain, took a trade-in of dubious value, it sent it to this "wholesale lot" for auction. Three dozen men, dealers, identified by little white squares pinned to their shirts or jackets, gathered there every auction day. The squares bore one- or two-digit numbers, identity tags for the bidding process. Most of the dealers came in the company of wives, assistants, or sidekicks whose chests did not bear numbers of any kind.

Every Tuesday, auction day, Labor-4-U dispatched eight people to drive cars at Automax; several times, I was one of the eight. The ticket drew three types of workers. Part-timers who owned vans or roomy cars volunteered for the Automax job because they could usually find three or four passengers, collecting from each. Women took the ticket because it was open to them. Young men went to the auction hoping for a chance to drive an exotic car—a Hummer, a Ferrari, and once, even a Lotus.

The mechanic wore a blue company uniform. A name tag on his chest said "Hernán," so I addressed him in Spanish. He was a Dominican immigrant. He told me that auction duty was rationed to mechanics on a rotating schedule because when they worked the auction, they were paid by the Automax sales department—at an hourly rate higher than that at the service department, where they were usually deployed. On auction days, two mechanics were dispatched to the yard, not to return for another six weeks.

Used-car dealers, most of them the owners of mom-and-pop lots, had been filtering into the yard and to the western side of the shed, where Automax provided doughnuts and soft drinks. The dealers stood in knots. Some chatted in English, some in Farsi or Arabic.

The man with the pencil-thin mustache had heard our Spanish conversation and joined in. He was an immigrant from Monterrey, he said.

Monterrey is Mexico's industrial capital, home to its steel, glass, and cement industries. In the region surrounding it, Monterrey's inhabitants are notorious as stern, tightfisted types.

So infamous is its reputation that in outlying areas, if one wants to say, "He's from Monterrey," one folds a fist to an elbow, stretches the other hand flat, and taps the elbow of the folded arm; *codo*, or "elbow," is slang for "cheapskate."

Monterrey's signature landmark is Saddle Mountain. A popular folktale explains its saddle-like dip: Years ago, one of the city's founders climbed that mountain, but when he got to the top, he dropped a silver peso. It fell into a crack, so he dug up the mountain to retrieve it.

In my experience—and I once lived there—the people of Monterrey don't take much offense when their reputation is cited, because, as they'll point out, it was Monterrey's tightfisted industrialists who a century ago made the town an industrial capital, ostensibly the most prosperous city in Mexico.

I razzed the Monterrey dealer about coming to the auction in search of cheap inventory, but our conversation didn't last long, because the mechanic and I were called to our tasks.

Hernán's job was to get the cars running, and sometimes, to give them CPR. On its windshield each car carried a number that indicated its place in the order of sale, and also a warning. Scrawled in yellow, most of the warnings said "Over 100,000," but some also said "Engine needs service," "Tranny needs service," or "Odom inop." Many of the cars wouldn't start. The two mechanics walked the lot with a jump-start machine.

Most of the cars hadn't been cleaned. Their steering wheels were sticky and their interiors stank of mold or rancid food. Spare change often lay on the front-seat consoles, and Labor-4-U drivers pocketed it when they could. But usually, the coins were sun-baked in a gooey residue of spilled soft drinks.

A few of the cars were clean and their motors, tight—a pleasure to drive. We didn't often find loose change or stray earrings in those.

Once we got a car started, we laborers drove it into a line of four or five vehicles to wait its turn on the auction patch. Some of the dealers had already walked the lot, noting the numbers on the vehicles that were of interest to them. But at least half of them wanted a second look. They streamed toward our line, crowding in front of and around our cars as if we were dignitaries in a third-world parade.

In summer months, like buyers looking into a horse's mouth, they stuck their hands inside our cars to test air-conditioning output. Sometimes they put their noses to the edges of the hoods. They took pleasure in cars that made no noise and had leather seats, and a few were dense enough to ask us, "Does it run okay?"—we, who had driven the cars about fifty yards! I once drew a red Porsche that was gaveled out at $23,000, but most of the cars sold for $2,000 to $5,000.

When our turns came, we drove onto the twelve-foot patch, auctioneers to our right, dealers to our left. At the conclusion of an auction spiel, an Automax employee signaled us by tapping the hood of the car with a short length of garden hose. Then we drove north out of the shed and circled to return the car to its place on the wholesale lot.

At mid-morning during the auction that day I drew a ten-year-old Cadillac. As soon as I started it, smoke began to drift out of the right side of its hood. I drove it into line, and its engine died. I restarted it and it died again. I started it again, and it died again. The wispy smoke frightened me and I didn't understand why the engine was dying, so I signaled Hernán. He stepped up to my car, glanced at the smoking hood, and told me, "It's just oil burning."

"But the car is dying," I said.

"Turn it off and don't turn it on until you have to go forward," he instructed.

I did as he told me, but when I got to the auction patch, the car was billowing again. Putting the best face on the situation, an auctioneer told the crowd, "This car has a lot of mileage. Its transmission slips and it smokes—but other than that, it's a fine car!" The dealers laughed, and one of them bought the Caddy for two hundred dollars; the rule was that every car would be sold, no matter what price it brought.

Once we returned a car from the auction shed to its place on the parking lot, we had to determine, according to the big number on its windshield, which car was next to be sold. Then we scurried to it and moved it into line. I was on the eastern edge of the lot, scanning the numbers, when I heard a crash. A couple of other Labor-4-U workers were in the area. We all froze, wondering which of us was to blame.

The lot was unpaved and had once been covered with gravel, most of which was now pressed into the ground. But near the fences, the gravel was thick. Mildred, a middle-aged woman incongruously attired in her Sunday best, had been parking her car, its nose toward the fence, and hadn't stopped. She'd hit a guard railing that stood in front of the fence. The rest of us rushed over. She was unhurt, but the bumper area of her car was crushed and the hood was wrinkled a bit.

Our supervisor from Automax, a stout white man in his early thirties, was on the scene in seconds. He was out of sorts, telling Mildred that reaching for the brakes with her foot, she'd hit the gas pedal instead. She claimed that the car's brakes had failed. A half-dozen of us collected around the pair. The car's front wheels were dug into the gravel, a sign that she had been braking, one of us argued. Before a dispute could erupt, the foreman—badly outnumbered!—said that he'd overlook the mishap if we'd "keep the show on the road."

All of us went back to our jobs.

On each auction day, as soon as all of the cars were sold, the dealers went to an Automax office on the highway, wrote checks for their purchases, and filtered back to the wholesale lot. A few merely got into their newly bought cars and drove off, but most, perhaps wise to what they were buying, had come with tow trucks.

We laborers boarded an Automax van for the ride to the main trade-in or retail lot, about a mile away, where cars awaiting service, cleaning, or auction were parked. In a series of trips over an hour's time, we'd drive a new supply of questionable cars to the auction yard, ready for the next sale day.

On the retail lot, we always trailed behind the Automax supervisor as he unlocked the trade-in cars. When he approached a car, someone would yell, "Mine!" The cars we chose sorted us into demographics of a rough kind. Women usually took clean, compact, late-model sedans. Older men looked for the protective bulk of SUVs and vans, while the hot-rodding youngsters went for sleek, sporty models with throaty engines. Some of us dreaded driving these unfamiliar vehicles, especially because we had to cross a four-lane highway, but the young men sped away like fugitives, radios blaring.

That day, on my first run from the retail lot back to the wholesale lot, I spotted the Monterrey dealer with Hernán and an Automax clerk, all three bent over the front end of the car that Mildred had wrecked. Other drivers hadn't arrived from the retail lot, so, rather than merely waiting for them and the van, I went to see what was happening. The damage, everyone had concluded, was not substantial. Its radiator was unharmed, its hood could be straightened and repainted, and a junkyard bumper could simply be bolted into place, the guy from Monterrey was saying; half a day's work and five hundred dollars in expenses would restore its damaged parts. He had won the bidding, and was keeping the car, he said, because, "We bought it for twenty-two hundred dollars, but after that lady wrecked it, they said they'd let us have it for nine hundred!" The car shark from Monterrey had lived up to his heritage, I thought.

On our last trip to the trade-in lot, we found ourselves with only one car to drive. I piled out of the van first because I was sitting next to its rear door. Reggie, one of the hot-rodders, a young black man in his twenties who was clad in a white undershirt and jeans, followed me. The vehicle was a green Jeep Cherokee.

"You or me?" I asked.

"It looks like your style, not mine," he said.

Our supervisor unlocked the Cherokee, but on the passenger side. Handing the keys to me, he said, "You'll have to get in on this side, because it doesn't look like the other door works."

I crawled in and reached for the driver's-side door, which seemed a little ajar. When I touched it, it fell open. I pulled it shut, but its latch wouldn't snap. I told the supervisor that I wasn't driving a car whose door might swing open on the road. He examined the door and fooled with its locking mechanism, but couldn't get it to stay closed either. So he told Undershirt and me to return to the van.

But Undershirt wasn't returning. Saying that he had once been a weekly-ticket man at Automax, he began to tinker with the door's mechanism, and after a couple of minutes, he said that he'd managed to get it to stay closed. I crawled back into the car from the passenger side and tested the questionable door. It held. Then I turned the key in the ignition. Nothing happened. The Cherokee's battery was dead.

It was a little past noon, close to the four-hour limit on our tickets. The supervisor decided to return us to the wholesale lot, where our drivers had parked their cars. Since the Automax lot lay in the exurbs, we always had time to banter during our trips there.

Because day laborers' lives are chaotic, because they don't own houses or live long in one place, and because some have criminal records that disqualify them from voting, political affairs were rarely mentioned in drive-time or idle-time talk, even during Obama's presidential election year. But one morning, when a political advertisement flashed across the television screen at the labor hall, I heard somebody seated behind me shout, "Vote for the brother!" A few people muttered assent, and that was the end of it.

Only one of our number could be counted on to bring up politics, a guy whom I nicknamed Captain America. He was a handsome white guy, thirty-eight, who, though he wasn't big, was powerfully built. With shining green eyes and hair hanging low around a sunburned face, I thought that he looked like the Jesus of the portraits, in army fatigues anyway.

Captain America rarely took a seat in the hall, preferring to hang out on the front porch, smoking and looking for a chance to preach his brand of "patriot" politics. His favorite entree was the military, which, he proclaimed, all of us needed to save our world from evil. I never heard him claim combat credentials, but he was quick to remind everyone that he'd served in the army fifteen years before. He sometimes lectured about such things as the forms used for discharges, the proper military name for a duffel bag, the numbered regulations pertinent to its use, and the legal differences between desertion and going AWOL.

Captain America was unusually literate. He carried books in his backpack and liked to recount the dark conspiracies that their pages revealed. He didn't have to tell anybody that if he were to vote, he'd have voted for the Libertarian Party, or maybe for John McCain.

He fancied himself an independent man, like Republicans and Green Berets. He detested homeless shelters, food stamps, and all forms of government. He was proud to say that he lived in a campsite whose location he wouldn't reveal.

One morning he reported to the hall wearing a white T-shirt that bore, on both its back and its front, an image of the Confederate battle flag. Maybe no one else noticed; not a word was said.

The men at Labor-4-U didn't dislike Captain America, despite his soapbox posturing, because labor-hall life was more complex than that. Those who had worked with him said that he carried his end of the load. They didn't mind working with him, they said, though they sometimes wished that he'd keep his mouth shut.

They weren't referring to his political views.

Captain America had a reputation for getting into wrangles about the proper methods of doing jobs. He always saw not an easier, but a more efficient way to perform a task, his coworkers complained, without denying that sometimes he was right.

One morning a rumor that he had been fired made the rounds on the porch. The story—or slander—could only have come from our managers, because it said that he'd been fired on a one-man ticket at a night job. He had gotten into a fistfight with a supervisor, the story went.

About a week later, Captain America showed up on the porch again, smoking as usual. I went to ask him about the rumor. He admitted that he'd been fired, but said that he'd only gotten into an argument, not a fight, and that his foreman had been a twenty-eight-year-old Nigerian—as if that justified whatever had ensued.

Captain America said that he was appealing his firing to the national office of Labor-4-U, on the grounds that his innocence was patent because he had a good record with Labor-4-U in three other towns.

As he was relating his case, Dolly and Stella came outside for a cigarette break. "You've been terminated and you will have to leave the property," Stella said. Captain America raised his fingers to the brim of his cap, nearly bowed, and calmly intoned that he would do "whatever you order, ma'am." But as he traipsed away, he turned toward them and said, "I am talking to the national office about this, and you will hear from them soon."

Those of us who knew him were waiting for him to add, as per MacArthur, "And I shall return."

I didn't hear anybody mention politics for weeks after Captain America left, until the day that Mildred wrecked the car. As we were driving back to the hall, someone brought up the subject, though not in the Captain's über-alles style.

I was sitting in the second or third seat of a van. The driver and a man sitting in front of me, both African American, had been talking about wayward friends who had become prisoners in the Drug War.

Driver: "You know, I just know that the only reason Bush went into Afghanistan was so he could get control of that heroin they make there. You know all of those guys are making plenty of money off drugs!"

Passenger: "Yeah, he was wanting to bring those drugs in, not keep them out. Just so he gets his cut, that's all he cares about."

Driver: "They're all making money out of drugs. You can believe that!"

Passenger: "Ain't that a fact! Why, even that Clinton was up to that kind of thing. Why else do you think a white man would move to Harlem, if he wasn't getting into the drug business!"

Everybody in the car broke into laughter, pleased to see a politician unmasked. Nobody mentioned Hillary, Obama, or McCain.

We reached the hall about one. Our tickets paid $6.46 an hour. That meant that our gross earnings were about $26, from which those of us who were car-less had to pay $5 to $6 for a ride. Most of us had signed in at the hall within minutes of six that morning: We had spent seven hours in pursuit of $20 in net wages. Those among us, especially the women, who were desperately in need, might have been willing to argue that we'd been gainfully employed. But I think that the hot-rodders understood the circumstance best. The Automax was a job, but just for fun.

7

RIVALRY AND THE FLU

Our ticket was for a cleanup job at a fancy-name seafood restaurant under construction in a building a stone's throw away from an upscale shopping mall. The fish emporium was a floor above ground, and accessible from the mall's second-story parking lot or from the ground—where the portable restrooms for construction grunts were located—via an elevator or a flight of thirty-seven stairs. Power hadn't been supplied to the elevator, and never is, while construction was under way. As soon as I arrived, I knew that my arthritic knee was in for a test, but I wasn't worried about my lungs.

That day was a Thursday. I was dispatched to the job with two men I already knew, a burr-headed, fortyish white named Donald, and Gary, a fiftyish black with a voice as smooth as velvet.

I had introduced myself to Donald while I was on the culvert plant ticket because its regular workers told me that he'd worked there, painting, for six months. Gary I knew because we'd worked at a drugstore, scrubbing floors, dusting shelves, and carrying empty boxes out of an attic, all to prepare for an inspection by regional officers of the chain to which the place belonged. What I didn't know was that Gary and Donald knew, and disliked, each other. In their rivalry, both wanted to claim me as an assistant.

The jostling began in the labor hall. Gary told me that the job required steel-toe boots, which I had never bought. I checked out a pair at the labor hall's desk, but I didn't like them. Those it issued to everyone were rubber boots with steel toes, and rubber boots are clunky. Besides that, the hall's inventory of loaner footwear began with boots a size bigger than my feet. We took a city bus to the job site, and when we reported, I noted that white-boy Donald was wearing mere athletic shoes. I stashed my rubber boots in the foreman's office.

The place was crawling with workmen of several trades. Plumbers were connecting two rows of steel sinks in an expansive kitchen. Sheetrockers from the Mexican states of Guerrero and San Luis Potosí were hanging and taping in a back room and in hallways, beneath electricians on A-frame ladders. By mid-morning, a crew of craftsmen from a thousand miles away had begun cutting and gluing thin sheets of a blond wooden veneer to the Tudor-style mock arches in the ceiling of the main dining room.

How long the crews had been at their jobs I couldn't tell, but from the look of the trash barrels that stood in the corners of every room, my guess was that it had been two weeks. They were overflowing, and while I did not sense any foul odor, I noticed that dust had collected atop the cups, food wrappers, cigarettes, paper towels, and bits of construction detritus that encircled them on the floors. Empty and half-empty soft drink cups sat on every windowsill. Expended tubes of calking; lengths of electrical wire, conduit, and copper tubing; and cartridges of nails from electric and gunpowder-driven hammers were underfoot. It was as if we'd walked into the place half an hour after an explosion.

The foreman's explanation for our presence, that his superior was flying into town that afternoon, reminded me of the adage "Every boss has a boss." But my take on the disorder was that the tradesmen had turned into either pigs or divas who thought that maid service came with the gig.

"Pick up a broom. That's your time card," Gary told me. I did as he said, and followed him into a back room where electricians were working. With gloved hands we lugged trash barrels to a Dumpster on the second-floor parking lot, collected cups and wrappers from the windowsills, then began the dusty task of push-brooming the floor. Gary eased into a hallway, sweeping, and in an instant Donald appeared, telling me to help him on a breezeway by the stairwell outside.

I followed him, laid aside my broom, and helped him move steel tubes from beneath scaffolds into orderly piles on the concrete floor. Someone came from inside, and warning us that the scaffolds weren't anchored according to OSHA standards, asked us to climb and dismantle them. I told Donald that I wasn't ascending, even though the scaffolds were only ten or twelve feet tall. It wasn't my knee that bothered me so much as the idea of risking a fall because of someone else's negligence. Donald went up and handed components down to me. I stacked them on the breezeway.

As we worked, Donald began telling me his story, a tale that I had difficulty following. His parents, he said, were educated folk with two other sons who were professional men. But he'd found his own career as a flea-market man.

His big success, he claimed, had come a couple of years earlier when he'd bought the mother lode of stuffed-toy Beanie Babies at a price that enabled him to undersell competitors at a weekend venue. The flea market required vendors to lease booths for six months, with rentals paid in advance, and he'd renewed his lease only a couple of weeks before ominous events began. Police officers in the suburb where he lived began to stop him on the streets and to keep watch on the apartment where he lived.

They'd even sent an undercover agent into his house, a woman he had met during the months he was working at the culvert plant. She was a lesbian, Donald was sure, but one night she had come to the door of his apartment, begging a place to stay until morning. He had demanded that she empty her purse on his coffee table to show that no recording device was inside. In the process of doing so, she had taken out her driver's license and laid it before him.

"From the way she put it there on the table, I could tell she was a cop," Donald told me.

I asked him what he meant, and he gestured as if laying something on a low table. I couldn't fathom anything from his pantomime.

After passing an uneventful night on his couch, the woman had disappeared from his life again, but by deftly asking people who might know, he had discovered a connection. An assistant chief of the suburban police force was related by marriage to one of his Beanie Baby competitors, and the lesbian was cooperating in their plot to ruin him because she was dating a man on the same police force who had drug-use information against her.

In fear for his life, Donald had abandoned the Beanie Baby business and flea markets altogether, but had recently completed his own investigation of the plot, lacking only a few details, and soon planned to take his findings before the state attorney general, he said.

I decided that Donald was scientifically paranoid, and to break the chain of his revelations, excused myself to descend to the bathrooms on the ground floor. When I slowly but painlessly scaled the thirty-seven stairs to the breezeway, Donald had wandered off. I resumed sweeping and seconds later was relieved when Gary appeared, motioning me into the main dining room, where he said he needed help.

A pattern was emerging here: When Gary was out of sight, Donald recruited me, and vice versa. I was a pawn in their dominance games—and I didn't care. My strategy was to obey any order either man gave me, as long as the two weren't in the same space when the order was given.

The specialists who were working in the main dining room cut their veneer with razor-bladed knives and let scraps fall to the floor. Fair enough, I thought. But when they went to work with their glue guns and pressed the veneer into place, globs of glue rained down. It wasn't their fault, but the globs were wet and slippery when they hit the floor—a hazard to people traversing the area—and we couldn't let them dry, or else scraping them off the floor would be tough work. So we swept and toted trash and kept cardboard sheets in view, for scooping the blobs away as soon as they hit. It was frantic work in a room swirling with dust.

At lunch, Gary befriended me. He led me across the second-story parking lot into the mall, where to my surprise, nobody hassled us, dusty and glue-spotted as we were, as we walked to a food court that I hadn't known about. At a kiosk that I would never have noticed, but whose offerings Gary knew by heart, we bought cups of iced tea that the proprietors refilled for free. Then we dined like gentlemen, surrounded by matrons and collegians who pretended not to notice scruffy us.

As we conversed, Gary told me that he came to the labor hall only for a second income because his occupation was buying and selling cars among his friends. I ignored his tally of vehicles bought and sold until he spiked it with a promise. That very afternoon, he said, his wife would deliver to the parking lot a five-year-old Lexus that was among his wares. I wouldn't have to ride a bus to the labor hall, and he wouldn't charge for our return, he said.

We went back to work, and during the afternoon, Gary called me away from a task Donald had given me, or Donald claimed me from a room where Gary had placed me, at least three or four times. The worst of it was carrying sections of steel I-beam from indoors to the back of the foreman's pickup. The foreman called all three of us to do the job, and I had to decide, with each beam, which of the two I'd assist. Maybe once or twice Donald and Gary shared a beam when the boss was watching, but they tried to avoid each other, even standing aside, doing nothing. I made almost twice as many trips as the other two simply because I didn't care who was on the other end of my beams.

True to his word, when quitting time came, Gary flashed the keys to a Lexus that was awaiting us in the parking lot. As he unlocked its doors, he offered me the shotgun seat and told Donald to get in back.

Late that evening, I began to feel awry. By morning I was coughing phlegm and running a fever. I was unable to go to work, and for the next three days I was flat on my back with something like the flu. I didn't connect the onset of my illness to anything, but the following week when I returned to work, I remarked about it to Gary.

"Oh," he said. "You must have breathed in too much dust. That's just part of cleanup work."

Nobody in the seafood joint had been wearing a dust mask, but I resolved that in the future, I wouldn't do cleanup work without one again.

8

Flagging

As soon as we piled into his car, the driver told us that he didn't allow smoking inside. We shot looks at one another: Who is this guy? Who does he think he is?

Only beer is more popular than cigarettes in day-labor ranks; 80 to 90 percent of its workers drink, 40 to 50 percent smoke.

Though we could see why the driver was laying down the law—his car was a spotless 2006 Mitsubishi Lancer—it made us wonder why he was at Labor-4-U.

He was a wiry African American in his twenties who spoke, not with a working-class accent, but like the child of teachers, insurance agents, or corporate drones—educated people. I took him for a student or office worker, fallen on hard times.

He was driving us to a construction job that, one of the labor-hall managers had said the day before, was "way out in the woods. Nobody can find it." Labor-4-U paid a twenty-dollar subsidy to any driver assigned to a destination more than twenty miles from the hall, and this job was thirty miles distant. But our driver didn't know about the subsidy. When one of us told him, he dialed his cell phone to secure a payment promise from Dolly.

Then he said that he wanted to return before the hall closed, just to make sure that the agency didn't welsh on its pledge. He didn't know what time the hall closed, nor did he know that Dolly wouldn't be on hand, because her shift ended about noon. The two males of the afternoon shift, we regulars knew, would be in charge by the time we finished work.

"You should have gotten that money up front," one of our number advised.

The young man was nervous, practically biting his fingernails, even though he was sure to collect twenty-five dollars from his riders.

Two carloads of us had been hired, for what tasks, we weren't sure. The client was a housing development firm with projects in a half-dozen states. Our car arrived by seven, on time, but when we showed, nobody was there. At seven thirty, when the second car found its way to the development, we were still unsupervised.

We took seats on a low stone wall around a traffic circle in what we thought was the center of the development, near the only building in sight, a five-thousand-square-foot model home, two stories tall. A few subcontractors filtered in, but another half-hour passed before we saw the first of the shiny white super-cab pickups that the developer's foremen drove.

Inside was a fortyish, short, muscular black man with a goatee and a white baseball cap which covered a "light bulb," or shaved head. "I need four of you guys with me," he shouted. I jumped into the super-cab.

We drove perhaps half a mile on paved roads through thick woods of slender trees. Lush carpet grass lined the roadways on every lane. The grass wasn't natural. It had been sodded, and here and there showed fresh tracks left by ride-around lawn mowers. The mowers had even scaled embankments that were ten feet high.

The foreman stopped his pickup and we dismounted, only to stand around for fifteen minutes more. Other white pickups whizzed past. Two or three stopped, carrying other members of our ten-man crew. Another pickup brought three or four Mexicans who worked for the developer, and one white man. About eight thirty Light Bulb told the gang of us to take tools from the bed of his pickup—shovels, spades, and picks. Fearing that my lungs couldn't handle the strain, I decided not to touch a pick.

With a spray can somebody had painted orange rectangular outlines along the edges of the pavements. Each outline formed a box about two feet wide and from three to ten feet long. Somebody with a big concrete cutter—we later saw the machine in use—had perforated the blacktop along the orange lines. The foreman wanted us to lift the pavement inside the boxes and to throw it into the "bucket," or scoop, of a backhoe, which showed up within minutes.

One of us ventured that the company wanted to put drainage pipes into the ground. But that wasn't the plan, Light Bulb said. The pavement had been in place for nearly a year. Soft spots had formed on its edges. Our job was to get rid of them. Once we had removed the boxes between the lines, he said, we'd repave the spots we had uncovered.

Henry Hilton, forty-two, a broad-faced, strapping black man whose cap hid a balding pate, had come in the car with me. He was a regular at Labor-4-U who, though he never mentioned any military experience, always wore a black T-shirt with a camouflage jacket, cap, and cargo pants. He had smooth skin, large, deep brown eyes, and—rare in day-labor ranks—a full set of unbroken, straight teeth. He could easily have been a model for the dutiful soldier of army recruiting ads.

He claimed to have a working wife and five children, including two elementary-age daughters, though whether all lived under one roof, I never bothered to ask. From other jobs I knew that he was competent and took on more than his share of any task, yet never complained. Others were as wary of the picks as I was—they cause lower back problems—but Henry took one anyway.

While we were waiting, I had chatted with the white man from the developer's crew, a guy named Terry. He stood perhaps six foot three, taller than most workers, but that was only the half of it. He was big-boned and stout, strong enough, and big enough, to carry a refrigerator on his back. A basketball would have been like a softball to him, so broad were his hands. Had he been bearded, somebody would have nicknamed him Paul Bunyan; had he been black, they'd have called him John Henry.

Terry had been telling me his story. He came to work for the developer, he said, after leaving a neighboring state at the end of a short career as a tradesman.

"I worked in glass," he said. "My older brother, he worked at a glass place in our hometown, and I got on because of him. They did mirrors, doors and windows in houses, even some windshields and auto glass. I got to be pretty good at cutting glass, mainly for doors and windows, but it was my brother who knew it all. It was pretty easy," he confessed with a grin. "A lot of times my brother would send me down to the store for a six-pack or a twelve-pack and I'd bring it to the shop and we'd sit in the back, just cutting mirrors to make crosses, things like that. The owner was pretty old and he and his wife weren't around the place too much. We pretty much, you know, did as we pleased. But then the owner died, and his kids, well, they sold the place. That brought in new management and they made some changes, you know."

His brother was spared, but the new owners sent Terry packing. He had caught up with the developer's superintendent, five hundred miles away—the greatest distance he'd ever traveled—and had been working with him since, going from exurb to exurb, an itinerant laboring man.

Light Bulb split both the Labor-4-U and developer's men into two groups, one on each side of the backhoe. For the next hour, we repeated a procedure. Henry stuck his pick into one of the lines and raised its block of pavement, which was about two and a half inches thick, a few inches above the ground. A couple of us slipped our shovels beneath the portion that Henry raised, then pried up too. Usually the slabs broke into pieces as they rose. When that happened, a gloved worker—or Terry, gloveless—carried a piece, if it was less than three feet long, to the backhoe alone. Pieces bigger than that, or whole sections, required two gloved men—or Terry.

Without any discussion, we spontaneously traded places from time to time; those who had been carrying took shovels, and those who had been shoveling carried pavement. But nobody reached for Henry's pick. After he tired a bit, Terry took his place.

Ultimately, a Bobcat came. It had a small scoop affixed to its arms, and on the front end of the scoop were three or four sets of steel teeth.

Pulling at his controls, the Bobcat driver slipped the teeth into the perforations around a block, then raised it, just as Henry and Terry had done. They didn't have to wield a pick anymore.

Over the next couple of hours each of our two crews "popped the pavement" on more than fifty boxes. We were progressing faster than he expected, Light Bulb said. Before long, three or four foremen in white super-cab pickups—lords on white horses, it seemed—split our two crews into smaller work details scattered over half a mile.

Perhaps because of my age, Light Bulb called me into his pickup and drove me to a place where the road became a divided avenue. An almond-shaped island about a hundred yards long lay between its lanes. The island rose and fell over a knoll. Limestone boulders as big as cars sat in the middle of the island, beneath skinny twenty-foot hardwoods. To my eyes, the scene looked more like something from a national park than a housing development. I imagined rustic mansions on one- and two-acre lots, each home nestled in the woods.

"These places, are they going to have big lots, maybe even ponds?" I asked Light Bulb.

"Huh! The lots are sixty by twenty," he said.

Light Bulb dropped me on what I took to be the eastern end of the island, handed me a small flag of orange plastic netting, and told me to keep vehicles from entering the road's westbound lane. It took a while before it dawned on me what the job of flagman—to prevent head-on collisions—implied. If I flagged vehicles into the eastbound lane, somebody had to halt traffic that might be entering from the other end of the island. Scanning the area, I noticed a figure with a flag like mine on the opposite end.

A couple of crews, mostly of Labor-4-U men, were working in the eastbound lane. Backhoes brought them granular asphalt—pebbles plus tar—which the men shoveled into the gaps or holes we had created. I could see the roofs of the backhoe cabins, and every now and then, a hard hat or two. But the rise in the knoll stood between me and them, and I couldn't see anyone's face.

In the idyllic setting where I stood, I could not imagine that traffic would be thick. But traffic there was. Not only were foremen in white super-cabs cruising the road, but people who appeared to be real estate agents were going by, their sedans carrying husband-and-wife duos. Landscapers and their crews, electricians, and plumbers also passed in vans. Every now and then an asphalt truck lumbered into view. Everyone stopped when I waved my flag. Looking westward, I would halt vehicles until my counterpart, whom I did not recognize, waved his flag, signaling that his end of the island was clear.

Before long a street-sweeping machine with a cigar-shaped brush came toward me. Its driver was a young Mexican wearing a face mask and a hood to keep the clouds of dust he created from getting into his lungs or hair. He drove his machine into the lane for which I had been stopping traffic and headed up the knoll, toward the other flagman.

Following the sweeper at a distance of about fifty yards was a white man on another sweeping machine. Behind them came a tanker truck spraying liquid asphalt in streams or lines about three inches apart.

A big machine that laid a blanket of granular asphalt onto the pavement followed the tanker, and after it came two men driving roller machines as big as one-car garages. What seemed to be miles of roadway were being resurfaced.

After I'd been flagging for an hour or two, a battered and bulky American sedan stopped beside the road. Inside were three of the Mexicans who had been popping the pavement. One of them, a light-skinned guy with black stubble on his face, was even shorter and thinner than me. Speaking in rough English, he invited me to lunch with them. I said that I'd brought a packaged dinner that I hoped to put in a microwave oven. Not even a cold-drink machine was on the premises, he told me. I got into the car, not knowing if I had permission to leave my post.

The three Mexicans, all in their thirties, were from different states: Jalisco, Michoacán, and Nayarit. The driver was a bronze-skinned young man who wore wraparound sunglasses. His car was making a grinding noise, and when we left the development and wheeled onto a highway, the noise became rhythmic—*harrumph, harrumph, harrumph*. I asked him if he thought his differential gears were going bad, but he said that the problem was that his automatic transmission "*liquea aceite"—aceite* means "oil," but the verb *liquiar* doesn't exist in Spanish: It is immigrant or border argot for "to leak."

The three were headed to a Burger King. When we got there, the little guy stood in line and ordered for the other two, who hadn't yet mastered fast-food English. All three were undocumented aliens, they told me, on salary with the developer at ten dollars an hour. Their only hope for establishing themselves in the United States and sending money home, one of them said, was overtime. "When we're lucky, we work sixty hours a week," he said.

We ate our lunch in a woody spot inside the development near the place where we'd begun popping pavement that morning. Several other workers, including my day-labor peers, were lounging on its grass or in cars.

Pretty soon Light Bulb drove up. I got into his pickup with the Mexicans. He delivered them to a foreman in a white pickup, but kept me inside, riding—for an hour and a half! He cruised from place to place, stopping to chat window-to-window with the driver of every white super-cab we met. I noted that all the other foremen were white except for one, who was bronze-skinned. It seemed that the client company had hired by a formula: one black and one Latino made for an integrated supervisory crew.

For a while Terry was riding with us. As he drove, Light Bulb told him that on Sunday, he had taken his first parachute jump. It cost him two hundred dollars. Ain't America great! he seemed to be saying.

About two thirty, Light Bulb drove onto a highway, and about half a mile later, turned off onto a dirt road. Soon we encountered a white foreman in a super-cab pickup. The two halted their vehicles to gossip. Three black guys from Labor-4-U were inside the other vehicle; Henry was one of them. After the two foremen had shot the breeze for a while, they told us to dismount and take tools—spades and plastic five-gallon buckets—from the white foreman's pickup. Light Bulb drove away, and the white foreman got out of his truck to instruct us.

We were standing atop a small bridge in relatively rough country; the shoulders of its road had not been sodded or smoothed. A muddy stream ran through the bridge's single steel culvert. Fences of black plastic netting had been raised on both sides of the bridge, and at places black gravel had been poured along the fencing's edges, both apparently to slow erosion. But water had washed some of the gravel into the muddy creek.

The foreman said that the washout had almost buried stones that nature had placed in the creek. Our job was to step onto those rocks, whose tops were still visible, and to shovel mud into our buckets, then to dump it on the far side of the black plastic fencing. When we had fully uncovered the stones, we were to wash them off with water from the creek.

We scratched our heads: The job didn't make sense. With a sigh that said, Yeah, this is really pointless, the foreman told us that ecological regulations required the company to keep the creek in near-natural condition. We descended toward the creek bed, and he drove away.

Two of the guys said that they weren't going into the creek for fear of snakes. I was afraid that carrying five-gallon buckets of mud would make me pant, so the four of us quickly came to an accord: Two would work in the creek, two would carry mud.

One of the guys said that he'd been on the foreman's crew before lunch, digging on the opposite side of the bridge. They had done their work slow and easy, and had finished in short order, as we would, he said. He was right: Within an hour we were done. We took our buckets to the road, turned them upside down, and sat.

The other three started conversing, just to pass the time, one on my left, two on my right, including Henry Hilton. All three were in their late thirties or early forties.

Earlier in the morning, while we were waiting at the stone wall at the traffic circle, Henry mentioned that he'd worked on the site the week before, on a four- or five-day ticket. While working that ticket, he had heard that the immigration service had raided the site and taken away twenty landscapers. Claiming that he had years of landscaping experience—something that was apparently true—Henry had filed an application for a job. But nobody had called him.

"That's because you've got the wrong name," one of them, a guy named Wilkins, said.

"Henry?" Henry asked with puzzlement.

"No, not Henry. You should be named Henry Sánchez!" Almost everyone laughed at that.

Then Wilkins discoursed on the subject of "the Mexicans." Mexican "fags" were "crazy about black men," he charged. Mexican couples had six to eight children, too many, and none of the Mexicans paid taxes. Mexican men were drunk drivers, a danger on the road, he added.

Wilkins, a very dark-skinned, chubby man, wasn't a stranger to me. I knew him from cigarette breaks outside the hall. I had once heard him tell how his "homeboy" had forced the closure of a competing labor hall by stealing its check-writing machine and giving checks to all of his neighbors. Wilkins had seemed to admire the thief.

He continued his rap about the failings of the Mexicans until he referred to their "circus music, you know, boom, ta, boom, ta, boom," voicing a *norteño* beat.

Everybody got a laugh at that.

"But I'll tell you what," Wilkins continued, now in a more thoughtful vein. "We're going to get even with them. Their kids, see, they go to school with white kids and black kids, and those kids are going to give the Mexican kids a kind of reorientation, you bet. They're going to lose their culture pretty soon. And only one thing can happen then. You think those kids aren't going to get into bed together? Hah! Those Mexicans, there's only one thing that can happen. They're going to get whiter or they're going to get darker—and with knotty hair too."

The three roared at that.

Discussion of Latino, and especially undocumented workers—competitors for bread!—I would learn, is almost as common as football-and-stage-star talk among day labor's men and women. It is not always hateful, and it's not racial, because all immigrants, even Africans, fall under scrutiny. "I don't like those Africans or the Jamaicans either," one of the women had told me. "They think they're more than you."

But foreigner talk in day-labor circles, as with most Americans, is usually uninformed. Once, Hulk and a couple of others were discussing Mexican laborers on the porch, and turning toward me, he remarked, "Those people, they must face a really hard time at home. What's wrong in their country? Who is their president—Castro?"

My fellow bucket-sitters kept jiving until they discovered, through chance remarks, that all of them were ex-cons. Wilkins claimed four terms—for breaking and entering, assault on a female, drug trafficking, and drunk driving—and I was afterward able to verify three of them. Henry claimed a drug conviction in the mid-nineties, the other guy, a drug offense after the century's turn.

But that discussion led to little besides a did-you-do-time-with-John? review between Hilton and Wilkins; the third guy had been imprisoned in another state. All three had found the experience distasteful, and they agreed that only masochists and fools would watch television's reality programs about life behind bars.

About this time the white foreman returned. He took us to an area where the others from Labor-4-U, plus a few employees of the contractor, had already gathered—one of the places where we'd popped the pavement. Backhoes were standing by, their buckets loaded with granulated cement. We took hoes and joined the others in shoveling the asphalt into the spots we'd cleared that morning. After we had laid about three inches of asphalt, a Mexican guy came with a vibrating machine that looked much like a gasoline-powered push mower. It compacted the asphalt. Then we'd shovel more.

The work wasn't fatiguing because most of the time we were waiting for backhoes to bring asphalt from waiting dump trucks. But the air was pungent because the asphalt was hot. We filled holes for about an hour, then got into the white pickups for a ride back to the traffic circle, where Light Bulb signed our tickets.

Our driver was still worried about his guarantee from Labor-4-U, which, until we told him, he thought included the money each of us had to pay. Still worried about the subsidy, he dialed his cell phone, but the hall had forwarded its calls to the agency's national headquarters. He was antsy during the whole drive back to town.

When we reached the hall, the clerk on duty gave him a check that included the subsidy. But our driver wasn't interested in learning where he could cash it right away.

"I have a bank account. I will deposit it," he told us.

That alone distinguished him from most of his peers.

"But the banks, they're closed," somebody warned.

"He can use an ATM, any ATM in the country," somebody else explained.

From our point of view, the driver had scored: He was paid his wage, the $20 subsidy, and another $25 from his passengers, a total of nearly $100.

But he wasn't impressed. Though we had a repeat ticket for the housing development job, we knew that we wouldn't see him again.

To boost his pay with fares, Henry drove to the labor hall the following morning in his wife's white junker, a Chevy Caprice with a rear window stuck halfway open. Wilkins sat up front. I took a backseat with Mickey, a thirtyish man, native to the West Indies, who always wore a black do-rag on his head. A white guy with shoulder-length hair got into the backseat after me, forcing me to the middle.

As on most morning runs, nobody said much: Talk shows on African American stations were the fare. We were at the job by seven thirty, but as on the day before, our supervisors hadn't shown.

Not until nearly nine did the second labor-hall vehicle arrive. Its passengers blamed their tardiness on the driver, a middle-aged regular known as the Teacher, whose late-model, luxurious van—dashboard, seats, and floors littered with Bibles and civics textbooks—was packed every day, so much so that he usually made as much from fares as from working.

The Teacher stood out in the labor hall, not because he'd been to college—though no one else had—but because of his appearance and his gait. He was matinee-idol handsome, more than six feet tall, with a café-au-lait baby face, heavy-lidded light brown eyes and gently graying temples. His gait—many tiny steps—was like that of a man wearing shoes too small for his feet.

The guys who came in his van said that he hadn't gotten lost in the woods, as the rest of us expected, but had simply driven too slow, fifteen miles an hour, they swore. I had ridden with the Teacher once or twice and I believed the charge. On one of the days that I'd been with him, he'd held a newspaper in one hand, reading local crime reports, while guiding the steering wheel with the other. Sitting in the front seat, I had implored the saints to guarantee our arrival.

The Teacher wasn't teaching anymore, he said, because for reasons he never specified, he'd been defrocked—lost his license. He claimed that he was studying for new tests and preparing for interviews with certification boards, but if that was true, he wasn't making rapid progress. For months he'd been at the hall every morning, ready to take on work as either chauffeur or toiler. On some days, he did nothing but drive because the hall sent him ferrying workers to job after job.

Prime assignments must have been in short supply that morning; one of the Teacher's passengers was Real Deal. Two or three guys groaned when they saw him, and it didn't make matters any better that he was accompanied by a sidekick, a yellow, swaggering young man with a heart tattooed beneath one green eye and a teardrop beneath the other. He claimed to be Deal's nephew.

I'd been talking with the long-haired white guy and with some Mexicans who worked for the contractor. The white guy said that he'd been a carpet layer who earned fifteen dollars an hour, and he bragged that he could lay seventy-five yards of carpet in an eight-hour shift. He had worked at renovating homes, not in new construction. It took a day to a day and a half to carpet an ordinary home, he said.

He showed me a form letter printed in blue, with a red-white-and-blue plastic card affixed. It was a food stamp card, he said, authorized for a month's rations, $162. He had received it by mail the day before at the mission where he lived, a place for drunks and druggies to dry out. Upon entering the shelter, he told me, he'd joined Alcoholics Anonymous and had since been sober for 103 days.

He was fifty-one, he said, and had for eleven years worked at carpet-laying for a man who "spent most of his time at the country club, drinking."

His boss was also a friend of cocaine.

"He had a camper trailer and one time we went to some car races together. He had a whole plastic bag full of cocaine in that trailer," the carpet guy said.

About 110 days earlier, he was working in a house when he heard a thump behind him. It was his boss, dropping to the floor—stone dead.

"They didn't do an autopsy or anything, but the EMS said that his heart just exploded. I think he must have overdosed," he told me.

He also said that he had an interview scheduled for a new carpet-laying job at week's end.

A long white pickup pulled up. I reached into my backpack to get ready for work, only to find my gloves were not inside. In nearly a panic I ran to the pickup to see if its driver had an extra pair in any of the three tool kits that sat in the truck's bed.

The driver was Cesar, the only Mexican foreman on the contractor's crew. The day before, I'd briefly chatted with him. He had told me that he was married to a Mexican American woman from a little town that, to his surprise, I knew.

He didn't have any gloves. "Don't worry about it," he said, as if doing me a great favor. "I'll put you to flagging."

I didn't like the idea, because as I'd discovered the day before, flagging is lonely work. I sauntered off to tell my troubles to the others. Terry, the Bunyanesque white guy, reached into his back pocket and came out with a set of cotton gloves. "My hands are pretty tough," he said, offering them to me. I took them and dashed back to show Cesar. Then I returned to the throng of my peers.

A few minutes later, as if they'd seen a signal that I hadn't noticed, everybody began moving out. I was with them when Cesar turned on the blinkers of his pickup, pulled over beside us, and told me to get in his cab. A short, stocky Latino perhaps my age was already inside. Cesar dropped him on one end of an island, me on the other. Not far away, the Labor-4-U men and a few guys from the contractor's crews, soon joined by backhoes, began filling holes that we'd popped the day before. Behind the backhoes came the street-sweeping machines, then the pavers, then the rollers. White pickups and yellow roadwork vehicles were moving in and out at both ends of the island.

My job was to keep cars out of the lane in which everybody was working. My counterpart was only a speck in my vision. I had to move toward the middle of the island to keep him in view, but from that vantage point, I couldn't stop anybody from entering my lane. We needed not two, but three flagmen, but since Cesar hadn't noticed the problem, I stayed where he had dropped me. When I allowed vehicles to pass, I merely hoped that they wouldn't meet others coming in the opposite direction. No mishaps occurred.

The crews finished one island, and we moved to another, which wasn't as long. After a while Cesar pulled up and drove me to a spot perhaps a mile away, about fifty yards beyond a knoll and twenty-five yards from a street that apparently led to an already-developed area; late-model cars came in and out. My job was to keep those cars from heading toward the islands where the paving crews were working. Traffic was light.

About noon Henry and Wilkins came driving down the road, on their way to lunch. They stopped and told me to get in. I protested that Cesar hadn't told me that I could leave.

"Who cares?" Wilkins said. "You work for Labor-4-U, not for the contractor."

I got into the car, not knowing who would take my place as flagger—or if anybody would.

Henry and Wilkins said that they'd been "patching," or filling holes, and that as on the day before, the work was easy and slow. Henry drove to a highway, turned onto it, and within a couple of miles, pulled into a supermarket parking lot. It was an upscale place: Its lot had spaces reserved not only for the disabled, but for "Shoppers with Children" as well. Henry pulled into one of those.

Inside I bought a packaged sandwich. Wilkins, with two dollars he borrowed from me, bought a can of ravioli, which he ate in the car while Henry drove to a convenience store for a beer. We took a longer route back so that Henry could sip from the can. He parked at the spot where we'd gathered at the start of the day. I took my flag out of the car and joined a clutch of Mexicans who were eating their lunches. We were chatting when Cesar arrived, a bit out of sorts.

"Why didn't you have those guys drop you where they found you?" he wanted to know.

I shrugged, got into his cab, and two minutes later, got out at a new location, about twenty-five yards from a highway. A white foreman was standing there, a flag in his hands. I took his place.

"Now I want you to keep everybody from coming in here," he instructed, motioning with a hand toward the highway. "If they're going to Gillis Woods, you can let them pass. If they're going into Oak Chapel"—he pointed away from the highway, back toward the interior of the development and the islands—"tell them to go two roads past the stoplight"—he pointed back toward the highway—"and to turn in on the construction road, Miller's Mill Lane."

I didn't know any of the landmarks he mentioned. I didn't know north from south. I didn't have any idea where I was.

"Where was that you said I should stop them from going?" I asked.

"Inside," he snapped, pointing toward the islands again.

Then he stomped to his pickup and left.

I glanced around, trying to get my bearings. I noticed a sign on a stone wall facing the highway. It read "Oak Chapel/Old Town Communities." As nearly as I could discern, the road on which I was standing led, behind me, to the islands in the interior of the development, which, it stood to reason, was named Oak Chapel; its development company was named Old Town Communities. It was my second day on the job and nobody had told me where I was working! A road that turned off only fifty yards behind me went to an existing development apparently named Gillis Woods.

Later I'd check Web pages to find out where I'd been. Oak Chapel, it turned out, was a sixteen-hundred-acre project slated to have a community center, soccer fields, tennis courts, nature trails, a middle school, a public library, a post office, and, the project's promotion page claimed, "mini-parks within neighborhood villages." Its homes were to be priced from $200,000 to $800,000—faux mansions on a faux woody estate, denuded and sodded to please, a village without a past.

The entry road on which I was standing had divided lanes. On one side, its south side, a paving machine was working. I stood in the road on the north side, flag at the ready.

When cars and vans came, I stopped their drivers, asked where they were headed, and did my best to repeat the instructions I'd been given. But some of the drivers were a problem. When they turned onto my road from the highway, I'd wave my flag at them, and some of them, noticing me, then drove past, as if they'd dismissed my presence.

Within half an hour, trucks laden with asphalt began to appear, and despite my instructions—"keep everybody from coming in"—I let them pass: They were obviously on their way to supply our crews. But I made a couple of mistakes, I suspect. One guy, who had a laptop open in the cab of his pickup, said that he was working, and I let him pass without asking whether he was headed to Oak Chapel or Gillis Woods. I made the same mistake with a landscaping crew.

Not for more than an hour did I notice that at the top of the knoll behind me another man was flagging—why, I couldn't tell. I didn't recognize him, but from then on, I looked for him before letting anyone pass. He would wave inward when the coast was clear.

A couple of hours went by. I stopped dozens of vehicles, even a sheriff's department patrol car.

But I was bored.

A little after three-thirty the other flagman signaled me, waving in a crossing pattern. I didn't know what he meant. Then he waved his flags over his head. I stood fast, feeling dumb.

He then waved in a horizontal motion, as if cutting his throat.

I got it: The machines were out of sight; our job was done.

I went trotting toward the knoll and caught him on its far side. He was a bronze man, from Mexico City's Chalco district, he said. He worked, not for the contractor, but for a paving company. I walked beside him for several hundred yards, until we came to one of the islands. Paving and rolling machines were on both sides of the avenue, and one side glistened with hot liquid asphalt. If the Mexican's job at our spot was finished, I thought, that didn't mean that I was done: My guys were beyond the paving machines, patching. Traffic would have to be stopped for them. I hustled back toward the intersection.

It must have been about four before I reached my post. No sooner was I back than a cream-colored SUV stopped in front of the stone wall with the "Oak Chapel/Old Town Communities" sign. Its driver slowly angled across the lane and turned in my direction. I flagged him to a stop. He rolled down his window, glanced at me, and rolled forward. I hollered, "Stop!"

He stopped. I took a look at him. He was about my age, chalky, hatless, and thin. Something about his complexion made me suspicious. Alky, I thought.

"Where are you planning to go?" I asked.

"To Oak Chapel," he said, a bit exasperated.

"Well, you can't get there from here right now," I said.

"I'm the general manager of Old Town Communities," he barked.

He may have actually said "general superintendent" or some such, but his words were clear enough. He was claiming to be the kind of person who, in Mexico, is called *el mero mero*, "the very very"—the Top Dog in Charge.

Or at least he said he was. I wasn't sure that he wasn't just an alky.

But I didn't ask for any identification.

"My instructions," I explained, "are to tell people to go up to Miller's Mill Lane." (I still didn't know where that was!)

He nodded as if he knew the place.

"If you're going in," I added, "tell them that if I'm not supposed to be flagging anymore, somebody should come and get me."

"You're doing fine," he said as he pulled away, headed toward the islands.

About 4:15 the sky clouded and turned dark. Drizzle began to fall, and I could feel a chill in the air. Impatient, I walked to the knoll, then down its far side, intent on getting to Henry's car before rain or quitting time. Near the first of the islands, Cesar drove up.

"I was coming to get you," he said apologetically. "That guy you talked to, he was the *mero mero!*"

We went back to the road where we had assembled in the morning and where Henry had parked his car. One of the Mexicans was operating a tamping machine. Backhoes were in the road. Several of the contractor's men were patching. Work was still under way.

But both carloads of Labor-4-U guys were standing aside. Real Deal was sprawled on his back in the grass, arms folded behind his head, as if he were napping. His shirt was open at the waist. He had a protruding navel, I noticed.

Wilkins was leaning on a rake.

"That's it! We're leaving at five!" somebody hollered.

"Yeah, that's it! That asphalt is going to be cold!" Wilkins shouted.

The contractor's men looked at them scornfully. A Mexican on a backhoe pulled up and killed his engine.

"Another truck is coming," he told us in English, his voice a command.

Real Deal jumped to his feet.

"There ain't no more trucks!" he bellowed. "We're done at five!"

"There's another truck coming. Larry is the driver," the backhoe man said.

"Well, fuck Larry! We're through at five!" another Labor-4-U worker shouted.

A hubbub ensued. I heard Real Deal yelling something about how he wasn't going to stand for "mistreatment." Intimidated, the driver stepped down from his backhoe.

"Well, at least I'm not paying for the truck," he muttered.

Just then the asphalt truck arrived. The backhoe driver remounted his machine and began to take a load with his bucket. Most of the Labor-4-U crew went to the holes. I grabbed a shovel and joined them.

At the hole where I was standing, Wilkins was raking and shouting at the same time.

"This shit won't do! It's cold!" he yelled. "It's supposed to be three hundred and fifty degrees, but it ain't more than ninety. These trucks, they are supposed to have warmers, but this one doesn't have shit."

"How do you know all that?" I interrupted.

"Shit, I used to do asphalt. I worked for a gypsy," he said.

"You still do!" someone chimed in, and everybody laughed.

Wilkins was right; the asphalt was chilled. It was hard to shovel and hard to rake because it stuck together in lumps. Even the tamping machine couldn't flatten it. Continuing was futile.

Real Deal called the guys from Teacher's van over to a long white pickup. They laid down their tools and went. The rest of us crawled into Henry's car and followed the pickup. We'd gone less than a quarter-mile when we met a foreman's pickup. It slowed. Henry stopped and handed our ticket to the white man inside. He signed it and we resumed our exit. Rain was falling fast.

Within half an hour, in the midst of a one-inch hail, tornadoes struck the area. We were out of the danger zone by then.

Because Real Deal and his buddies were riding with the poky Teacher, we beat them to the hall.

"How did it go today?" a young white dispatcher asked.

"It was easy, but we had problems," someone said.

"What kind of problems?"

"Real Deal," the informant said.

"Yeah," another of our crew added. "He was complaining all day, saying that he didn't work no concrete and he didn't work no asphalt either. He told them they were mistreating us, but hell, we were hardly working."

Despite the ruckus Real Deal and Wilkins had raised, all of us—from both cars—had been given repeat tickets.

Due to the storm, it was too wet to work the next day.

9

THE CELL PHONE

The first time we went outdoors, after stuffing the store with boxes, I was relieved to be outside. The place was driving me nuts. Though it had the word "gallery" in its name, that store was an artless place.

Located in a shopping mall that was a constellation of two- and three-store clusters, its exterior was of picture windows between walls of faux sandstone sheathed in bands of fake granite. Inside were three huge rooms of faux paintings in ponderous wooden and mock-gold frames; gargantuan mirrors; ceramic vases, elephants, and lions, all of them three feet tall; even a niche of dinnerware adorned in a skull-and-crossbones design. It was as if a mad scientist had taken the wares of a dollar store and run them through a magnifying machine.

As far as I was concerned, nothing in the store was worth stealing, let alone buying. Its only useful merchandise lay in a fourth room that displayed tropical-theme bedroom furniture from Indonesia and the Philippines.

Tommy—a wiry, dark-skinned, fortyish black with high cheekbones—and I had replenished the wares. We'd arrived in the company van about 7:00 a.m. A light rain was falling. At the back of the store we'd met the store's manager, Mandy, a fleshy young blonde who was a graduate of the business school at a nearby women's college. She was dressed in a T-shirt and khaki pants for unloading day. Within a few minutes a driver was turning and backing, turning and backing, to get his trailer in place. A college-age white guy, wearing short pants and a nylon knee brace like mine, jumped into the rear of the trailer, joined by a diminutive, jeans-clad white woman about the same age. The two began handing odd-shaped boxes to Tommy and me, on the ground, while the manager stood behind us, sometimes helping, but always carrying on a conversation with the young man about World Wrestling Entertainment personalities and scenes. It took us most of the morning to unload the truck, whose heaviest items, unwieldy boxed mirrors, came at the end.

As we unloaded we'd taken the boxes inside on hand trucks or dollies. In a storeroom we wedged boxes between shelves and along walls until, out of space, we stacked boxes in its aisles, walling ourselves out of it. Then, under the manager's direction, we'd taken other boxes into the showrooms, stacking them wherever we could. In the process, Tommy's dolly had struck one of the tall flower vases, sending it crashing to the floor. But it didn't break because that one, to our relief, was made of fiberglass.

A little before noon, the tiny white girl went to a fast-food outlet and came back with what she called biscuits for all of us. The biscuits had sausage, scrambled eggs, and yellow cheese between them; two or three of them were enough for a meal. While the regular employees gathered around a circular cashier's counter inside, Tommy and I went out back and sat down on a curb. That's when, while chomping on a biscuit and sipping a soft drink, he'd made his first cell-phone calls, maybe three of them. When he finished eating, he asked me for a cigarette. I went inside, where I'd left my backpack, in which I kept cigarettes, even though I rarely smoked anymore. When I returned, he was dialing his fourth call.

After lunch, the two of us, the manager, the knee-brace guy, and the tiny woman, along with a business-attired man we hadn't seen before, started opening boxes with blade cutters and unpacking the merchandise. The regular employees carried items to shelves; I noticed that each already carried a price tag.

Soon the floor was strewn with filmy packing materials and the remnants of boxes. Tommy and I stuffed the packing materials into transparent plastic bags six feet long, and stuck their cardboard sides into empty boxes, which we loaded onto a dolly to go outside. It took two of us to move them, one to push and the other to guide it and move aside objects in its path. When we reached the back door on our first trip, as Tommy tried to fit his load through its opening, cardboard tubes and braces spread out two feet on both sides of the dolly.

A trim young brunette, smartly dressed in black, appeared outside. She couldn't get through the door because of us, so she said in a chilly voice, "I think it's usual for you to move out of the doorway to let guests enter." We blinked. I pulled the door wide open and leaned toward the dolly, to help one side of it clear. When Tommy got through the doorway, the young lady went in. "I started to give that bitch the finger," he told me.

It's a good thing he didn't. Twenty minutes later, we discovered that she was an employee of that wonderful place.

Outdoors our job was simple and might have become pleasant. We had to guide the dolly to a set of interconnected, motorized Dumpsters. The one on our right had a door and, beside the door, a keybox and control buttons. The manager had given us a key. We opened the door, hurled our boxes in, and pushed a button. The floor of the Dumpster rose, crushing the cardboard flat, then delivered it onto a belt that ran into the Dumpster on the left-hand side. It was a slow and nearly noiseless process, and I was relieved to see that our boxes were apparently being recycled. I would have felt useful and nearly at ease if I hadn't had to do the job, on all of our nearly two dozen trips, almost by myself.

On each trip—when he came along—Tommy's behavior was the same. When we reached the Dumpster, his right hand went into his pocket for the cell phone. He dialed first one woman and then another, sweet-talking each in turn, with lines like, "I have, you know what I mean, a good heart. I mean, I'm a good-hearted person. It's just that, with some of these ladies, I sometimes have trouble because, you know, y'all are all so crazy!"

He didn't ignore our job, not entirely anyway. He stood, one hand to his ear with the cell phone, the other courteously grabbing slivers of cardboard and chucking them into the Dumpster.

Perhaps it's to his credit that one of the calls he made was to a blood relative, a cousin. I heard him giving her instructions on how to drive to a misdemeanor court. His guideposts were clear—references to railroad tracks, convenience stores, and stop signs. It was as if he went there every week.

"How come you know that place so well?" I asked him.

As he dialed a new call, he muttered something about having been in trouble when he was a young man. I later checked, and though the records showed no recent felony convictions, the late eighties had not been kind. In 1986 he'd been placed on probation for assault and robbery with a deadly weapon, and in 1987 he'd been sent to prison for eighteen months for escape, receiving stolen goods, and attempted felony theft.

Of course, after he had confessed to his past transgressions, I suppose he had to collect. He asked me for another cigarette and again I went inside to fetch one. It's not unusual, of course, for day laborers to bum smokes from one another, and sharing them is a gesture of friendship. But as a sign of respect, most day laborers offer a quarter for each of them, even knowing that payment will be declined. Tommy never reached into his pocket for anything but his cell phone.

I had to make some of the Dumpster trips alone because, between telephone calls, Tommy had developed a new scheme. It started when the manager, spying him as he made a call from inside the store, scolded him, though in a tentative and polite way. Five minutes later, when I was ushering a dolly loaded with boxes past the skull-and-crossbones niche, I spied Tommy in his sweet-talking mode—running a line on the manager. "Mandy, you are such a real person. I mean, by the way you treat us and the way you run this store, it shows that you really do care, not just about your job, you know, but about all the people you work with," he said.

A few minutes afterward, as I was unloading the dolly into the Dumpster, Tommy sauntered to my side, lowered his cell phone, and confided in me.

"I'm getting over on that Mandy, you know. I think I'm going to ask for her phone number."

After he said that, of course, he sent me for another cigarette.

About two thirty, Mandy assigned us a new task. One of the bigger boxes we'd stacked in the store contained a bed frame and headboard. It was our job to assemble it while she watched. Tommy kept trying to sweet-talk her, but when he did, she'd turn away.

About three thirty, when all the merchandise that the showrooms could hold had been unpacked and shelved, I locked the control box on the Dumpsters and returned inside, parking my hand truck in the now almost spacious storeroom. Picking up my backpack, I found Tommy, who had our ticket, negotiating with Mandy at the circular counter.

He was telling her that as nice as she was, she ought to give us credit for extra hours. Since we hadn't taken breaks and hardly took time for lunch, I calculated that we'd been on the job for 8.5 hours.

"How much should I give you?" she asked.

I was about to say "Ten hours" when Tommy spoke.

"How about nine and a half?" he said with a proud grin.

The manager did as she was told, and even checked a box saying that we had done a satisfactory job that day.

That morning, the Hulk had driven us to the shopping center. As we walked out the store's back door, it dawned on me that I didn't know how we'd return to the hall.

At last I was gratified that Tommy had brought his cell phone. He'd already called Labor-4-U, whose van was waiting when we stepped into the street.

10

A Lucky Guy

Sung was a figure that nobody overlooked, even though he usually came and went in a flash.

He was Asian American and short, even shorter than me, and though he said he was thirty-three, he looked ten years younger.

When he walked, he swung his arms and snapped his shins, as if to kick the brogans off his feet. He had a clean-shaven face with broad features, big brown eyes, and thick lips. His straight black hair, cropped into a burr, was evident only once in a great while, when he removed the white bandanna that covered it, Aunt Jemima–style.

Sung wore white sleeveless T-shirts and pale, baggy jeans that were too long for his legs. He was muscled, but in a smooth, thick way; his was not the chiseled look. He talked in a rapid-fire cadence, yipping more than speaking.

He was gung ho, a go-getter: Let's get ready to do some *work!* His age—youth means vigor—his attitude, plus his effervescence at 6:00 a.m., made him one of Dolly's favorites. She always gave him a ticket, first thing in the morning, every day.

One morning she called Sung to the counter with a white man named Jack Clemmons.

Jack's face was bony and angular. He had a pointy chin, dark, wavy hair, and pale blue eyes. He was a cracker, like me, slow-talking and slow-moving—not the picture that people have in mind when they say "bursting with energy." By all appearances he was in his late thirties or early forties and would within a few days claim to be thirty-nine, though he was probably older: I later found a listing with his name and birth date, age forty-seven, on an electronic roll of drunk-driving felons. He had been convicted once, a decade earlier.

He wore ordinary jeans and a long-sleeved, button-down shirt, a red baseball cap on his head. His facial expression, most of the time, was an empty stare, eyes downcast. When Jack wasn't deferential, he was lifeless.

A couple of minutes after she called Sung and Jack, Dolly called my name. I joined them at the counter.

Dolly leaned toward the other two: "How rough was that job yesterday?"

"Well, I guess you might say it was heavy work, but not too bad," Sung chimed.

She turned her eyes toward the cracker. He nodded slightly, as if a prayer had ended and it was time for everybody to say "Amen."

"Do you think he can do it?" she asked them, gesturing at me.

"Why not?" Sung chirped.

Jack shuffled behind me and I scampered to keep up with Sung as he led us into Labor-4-U's parking lot. He took us to a white 1998 Jeep Cherokee, which he said he'd bought only two weeks before. It was dolled up with chromed taillights and fancy hubcaps. Not a dent, not a scratch, was evident on its body.

The Cherokee is neither station wagon nor SUV, but something in between. Its trunk lid rose, coming to rest parallel with the ground, perhaps six feet below. Inside its trunk area sat one of those boom-box contraptions that hip-hoppers love—four speakers in a single cabinet about twelve inches wide, thirty inches long, and eighteen inches tall. The speakers faced upward, toward the car's ceiling. We tossed our hard hats and gloves into the spaces on either side of the noise machine.

Jack climbed into the shotgun position. Sung opened a passenger-compartment door for me, on the driver's side.

His car had cream-colored leather seat covers! Knowing the class of passengers he carried, Sung had draped them with nylon blankets.

Our assignment, which like the street-patching and flagging job would last several days, was at a public school seventeen miles from the labor hall. Drivers usually make a morning stop at a convenience store, and Sung always bought cigarettes, name-brand cigarettes, not off-brands like other Labor-4-U men. But in defiance of common custom and the unflagging charm of Madison Avenue, he showed no brand loyalty.

"They're all the same," he told me when, a few days later, I noted that he'd switched from mentholated to plain cigarettes.

"I look for the two-for-the-price-of-one deals," he explained. "Sometimes one brand is on sale, sometimes another."

On our drives to job sites, Sung played techno music, and sometimes light classical pieces. The speakers in the back of his car were out of whack, playing only bass notes, but Sung didn't mind. He'd crank up the volume, and every plastic part in the car—moldings, latch guards, and the like—would vibrate and hum. After a couple of weeks, prospering, he installed a black vinyl cover over the trunk area. When his music played, the cover pulsed in time to the speakers' blasts, a black flag of penury undulating in an electronic wind.

Sung was an observant driver, but during our time together he developed a habit of the oddest kind. His horn was not working when he'd bought the Cherokee, though he checked it by trying to sound it from time to time. One morning it honked, God knows why. For days afterward, about every ninety seconds, Sung would honk his horn just to make sure it was still in order. At six thirty in the morning, passing through a neighborhood whose residents were still sleeping, he'd honk his horn. At four in the afternoon, surrounded by a swarm of cars on a congested six-lane avenue, he'd honk his horn. Other drivers startled and glared, but he didn't notice. It was his horn, not public acclaim, that counted.

Our labor had been contracted to an HVAC, or heating, ventilation, and air-conditioning, firm. We worked from 7:00 a.m. until 3:00 p.m., mostly moving ducts from one place to another.

The school had been built in the late 1970s; dates were scrawled in chalk on concrete beams that had been exposed when, days before our arrival, other workers gutted its ceilings. The architecture of the buildings spoke of age too: earth-toned, one-story red-brick classrooms with flat roofs hidden behind dark green, sloping mock-mansard panels. Each building contained two or three classrooms and a structure called a pod. The pods stood as if at the lower ends of the spines of folding fans. Where the spines—breezeways—met, stood indoor theaters whose stages were two and a half feet belowground and were surrounded by concrete stair-seats.

Busy construction sites resemble battlefield camps. At any moment, a hundred or more men kick or loll about in the dust, some scurrying, some idle. As in a military camp, the men belong to small companies, each distinguished by a uniform. Most crews wear safety vests—some yellow, others orange or red, some with reflective strips running down their fronts or across the shoulders, a different vest for each crew.

Plastic hard hats are another element of the uniform, many of them carrying stickers emblazoned with corporate names or logos. Some crews wear goggles, usually because safety rules require as much. For the same reason, other workers wear earplugs or cover their mouths and noses with white paper masks.

As in military camps, on big sites, a tiered system of subordination makes intermittent idleness inevitable. Just as a soldier may not fire his weapon without an order, workmen are to do the task they've been assigned and nothing more. Their foremen, the lieutenants of the construction camp, often have to converse with the Big Brass, suppliers and superiors, up a chain of command that ends with the GC, or general contractor. When a task has been completed and foremen are in consultation, or when building materials—munitions—are not on hand, workmen either sham, or on big jobs, simply stand or sit, awaiting new orders. As military jargon would put it, their cadence—their motion and their rest—is set "by the numbers."

The hierarchical system is a good thing for workers, especially unfit men like me, because what it means in practice is that sustained exertion is rare. One works for half an hour, maybe an hour, and afterward waits for new instructions or materials.

Though we arrived a few minutes before starting time, crews from a half-dozen trades—plumbers, electricians, welders, roofers, drywallers, demolition men—were assuming their posts, perhaps two hundred, all told. By asking, first here, then there, Sung found our company's spot in the strung-out ruins and made contact with our foreman, Walter, a burly black man whose hard hat—a sign of rank?—was of the old "skull bucket" or engineer style, made of stamped aluminum, a two-inch flat brim in a full circle beneath its crown. He stood poring over blueprints at what was for him a table, a five-foot-tall air-conditioning duct with a sheet of plywood laid across its top. He looked a lot like an officer in a battlefield tent.

Walter was wearing nylon gloves like none I had ever seen. Their surface perfectly followed the contours of his hands, as if they'd been molded in place. Their fabric seemed thick, suited for heavy-duty work, but the fingers of the gloves were so pliant that he was using a pencil to check items on a list.

How I envied his gloves! Mine, of canvas and leather, were so clumsy and stiff that I couldn't put on my eyeglasses without taking them off.

Walter pointed us toward the northeasternmost spine of the site. The building he signaled had been reduced to a cavern, strewn with shattered glass and concrete rubble. It had two rooms, each about twenty by thirty feet. About seventy-five galvanized steel ducts stood against a wall on the littered floor of one of them.

The ducts were of a dozen sizes and shapes. The smallest were mere four-inch hollow cubes, the largest, as big as eight by eight by two feet. Some of the bigger ducts had inch-wide flanges on their top and bottom ends; some had flanges on only one end. Each duct was wrapped in transparent cellophane much like the kitchen product Saran Wrap. Each bore white stickers displaying its size in black type, plus information that neither Sung nor Jack nor I could understand.

The ducts had been built in an off-site shop and delivered by truck. We had to move them to a building that lay thirty yards west, at the next blade of the folding fan, the building where we'd encountered

Walter. Between them was a patch of moist ground, inclining upward three or four feet toward the building where Walter stood. The task ahead looked like a three- or four-hour job.

Sung bent forward, grabbed a big duct between his arms, and hoisted it onto a shoulder. The duct was as big as he was! He went walking out of a door-less doorway.

Jack and I looked at one another, both of us grinning, then cut our eyes around the room. Jack spotted a yellow hand truck and wheeled it to the ducts. I stepped up to a big duct and tilted it—it must have weighed forty pounds—so that he could insert the hand truck's base-plate beneath it. Jack started wheeling it out of the building and I followed, one hand supporting the duct so that it wouldn't tip over. Two of us were moving a piece that Sung would have handled alone.

Neither Jack nor I said anything, nor did anything need to be said. Our motions had spoken for us. We were older and smarter; we observed the rules of the game, the terms of the contract; we knew the name of the deal.

The rules were that our temporary employer, the air-conditioning company, had that day rented our muscle-power, a quantity of calories or energy, from Labor-4-U. The number of calories we were to expend, or the amount of wear and tear we were to endure, was nowhere measured or stated. It was a mystery: Call it x. When we reported for work, it became Walter's duty to extract from us at least x, if not x-plus, calories. And it became our duty to yield x-minus calories. It's a question of the intensity of labor. Jack and I were on the job as professional sloths, as x-minus men. Sung was giving his life away. A lot of younger day laborers do that because they mistake every job for a challenge to their virility.

The inclination of most older day laborers to exert themselves as little as possible is not precisely a matter of class consciousness, as Europeans might think. Casual workers know that they're mere grunts or, as the Mexicans say, *bueyes*—oxen.

But they don't think that's because any blameworthy system of exploitation is in play. Instead, day laborers believe in the irrational: The world is a jungle regulated only by luck. Some people are born prosperous and white, some are born poor or female; it's a matter of luck. Some were standing in the right place on that glorious day when cushy jobs were handed out, and some weren't—again, a matter of a lightning strike, blind chance. Some men luck into positions where they can get rich by exploiting the labor of others, and some don't, but if given the chance, even the unlucky would do the same as their lords. Nor do day laborers believe, like European workers, that forming unions or voting can change their circumstances. Laws or regulations can inspire countermeasures, but they can't for long override luck.

All that counts is what's ahead today, what's near at hand, this job site, that supervisor, the nearness of break time. Being lucky, for most of my peers, meant that you momentarily found yourself in the company of coworkers who didn't want to exhaust themselves and a foreman prudent enough to stay out of the way.

Without saying anything, when Jack and I returned to the building to pick up our second duct, we traded places. I took the hand truck and he steadied our cargo: "Turnabout is fair play" is another unspoken rule. Because of the incline between the two buildings, pulling the hand truck was harder work, at least for me. I had to stop midway on the incline to catch my breath.

Within an hour the three of us had moved the big ducts and stacked them side by side. Then we began with those of medium size, most of them four to five feet long, not more than two feet wide and two feet deep. Using the hand truck would have been superfluous, almost a boast of our laziness, so when Sung put one of these ducts over a shoulder and cradled another beneath his free arm, Jack and I hoisted one duct over a shoulder, but nothing under our arms. Then we hit upon a better plan: two guys to a duct, one on each end.

I am quite sure that Walter and his NCOs, the semiskilled workers on his crew, noticed that one Sung was worth as much as the two of us. But Walter neither objected nor gave any advice. Nobody said anything, because at day labor, most men won't tolerate lectures. On the big projects, a day laborer who shows up sober and doesn't sleep on the job is not going to be harassed or harangued or scolded, as long as he goes through motions that resemble work. On small jobs, overseers may "redneck" their laborers, but on full-bore projects, a good deal of the time, foremen and other bosses won't even know a worker's whereabouts.

By ten thirty that morning, the three of us had moved the rest of the ducts, and, because Sung started doing so, we had aligned them by size, big ones together, then the medium-sized and small ones. We reported to Walter, who asked us to stand a few yards away; he was conferring with a paunchy and balding white man in tan slacks and a blue business shirt.

Other crewmen were assembling the ducts we'd brought. Following blueprints, they hooked them together into one long, tapered rectangle, covered with aluminum-wrapped insulating material held in place by tape. With the help of a forklift, the men raised their assemblages to the concrete roof, where they bolted them to iron rods called "all threads." The rods had been screwed or drilled into the concrete, whether for the former ductwork or the new, I couldn't discern.

A tall, very black man with a thin, two- or three-day beard was ascending an A-frame ladder, a roll of duct tape and a can of mastic in his left hand. When he was midway up, another workman came to steady the ladder from the ground. The stubbled man put the duct tape and the mastic into the open end of the assemblage, then turned his back toward it, and climbing to the top of the ladder, lowered his brogans and legs into the rectangle's opening. Then he disappeared, crawling backward—suspended in the duct, ten feet aboveground. His task was to seal the assembly's joints from the inside.

My mouth dropped open. What if the duct were to give way? Falling ten feet inside a steel cage was not an accident I wanted to contemplate. No day laborer—except maybe Sung—would have accepted that job, I found myself thinking, glad to have my low-wage feet on the ground.

The man in the blue business shirt walked off and Walter pointed us toward the outdoors, west of the building. In a courtyard between it and the building on the next spine of the fan lay perhaps two dozen duct assemblies, bent and broken into segments of various lengths. The ducts had been tossed or carted there when the building was gutted.

Our job, Walter said, was to put those ducts into a red, topless Dumpster thirty yards away.

Sung, who took the lead, picked a small and a medium-sized duct. Jack and I grabbed a middle-sized duct each and followed him. Sung threw his ducts into the Dumpster and we did the same, repeating the process, time after time, for perhaps half an hour.

Then we realized that we had a problem: The Dumpster was already more than half full. It would not be roomy enough to hold the discarded ducts that remained.

"We're going to have to flatten these things," Sung said.

Jack and I looked at each other and shrugged as if to say, Who does this guy think he is, anyway?

Nobody had told us to flatten the ducts, and if we could fill the Dumpster, we'd probably get to wait until a new one came. And if a new Dumpster couldn't be brought that day, Walter would have to give us something else to do. Jack and I stood around, hesitant and mum.

Sung climbed into the Dumpster and began pushing and tossing ducts our way. We took them and, one by one, stood on them and stomped until they were flatter. Then we raised them to Sung, who stacked them inside the Dumpster, back-to-back like sardines in a can.

While we were doing this, the stubble-faced black guy—the hero of the hanging duct—appeared to tell us that lunchtime was nigh. He was acting as if he were our boss, but of course, we didn't mind: He was looking out for our interests.

Drivers decide where their crews go for lunch, so it was Sung's call. Playing techno music through his speakers and testing his horn, he drove us to a strip shopping mall a couple of miles away. A fried-chicken joint stood on one of its edges, next to a convenience store. Jack headed toward the chicken joint. I followed Sung, who spotted a Chinese restaurant. It was one of those dark, candlelit places with white tablecloths and a patronage of office-manager types. Its menu items started at ten dollars.

"Oh, do you want something to go?" its matron screeched as the two of us stumbled in, dusty and sweating from the sun.

Standing at the café's cash register, Sung scanned the menu, calm and cool. He ordered egg drop soup and white rice, and I followed suit. The tab for each of us came to $2.70, safely within the $3-a-lunch outlay that laborers usually observe. When we met Jack at the car, he was toting not only a box of chicken, but a plastic cup of iced tea—of halfgallon size! Having never seen such a mammoth throwaway container, I ran into the chicken joint to get one for myself, as much a souvenir of pop culture as to quench any thirst.

Being gentlemen, of course, the three of us didn't dine in the Cherokee. Instead, we returned to the school's parking lot and took our lunch at a picnic table in an adjacent park. Jack was elated. Smoking was forbidden on the job site: Children might see! Our Dumpster, the buildings, the whole work area, were behind hurricane fencing and yellow marker tapes that said "Authorized Personnel Only." And school was not in session. But the site was on school property, where the mere possession of cigarettes was a crime, and somebody had warned us to be on watch because busybodies sometimes cruised by the site. When we'd been told this, Sung hadn't complained, nor did he try to evade. But that morning Jack had more than once slunk into a corner of a courtyard to light a cigarette behind a stand of bushes. In the park, he could smoke like a free man.

Not long after lunch, having loaded all the other discarded ducts, we faced a huge assemblage, more than a dozen feet long and four feet wide. The three of us—Sung on one end, Jack and I on the other—could lift it six or eight inches, but carrying it thirty yards was out of the question. Jack and I cast our eyes around, wondering what to do. The thing was too big to hide.

"Come on, come on," Sung said in a voice low enough not to scold.

We looked at him, eyes wide open, wondering if he thought that the three of us could do the impossible.

"I'm pumped up to *drag* this thing," he declared.

Jack and I began shaking our heads, saying it couldn't be done— and that's when an idea came to me.

The assemblage was bolted together at various points. I went to the building where Walter and his crew were assembling and installing. From them I borrowed a ratchet wrench and a big screwdriver, then set to work to dismantle the gigantic thing. I wrenched for fifteen or twenty minutes, but the joints in the duct still didn't budge: Most of the nuts that I'd removed held rods that kept the ducts from losing their shapes.

Stripping the big duct of its insulation, Sung discerned that the monster was held together by folds in the metal at the ends of its components. He put the screwdriver to work as a pry bar, and in another five minutes, had broken the assembly to a manageable size.

At least he hadn't dragged it, I sighed.

While we were loading the pieces into the Dumpster, Walter came through with a hard-hatted white guy and a middle-aged Latino in tow. The two new faces had arrived with an open-air truck loaded with new ducts. They parked their truck by the Dumpster, and the three of us began duct-toting again, this time to a third building on the fan.

Other men were at work in this structure, gutting it. Some of them, with crowbars and straight-blade power saws, were pulling and cutting the steel frames that held doors and windows to cinder-block walls. Others were sweeping with push brooms. They and a fortyish woman, heavy with eyeliner, wore yellow safety vests and yellow hard hats with a logo on their fronts. They were workers from a demolition crew.

All of them were Latinos, even the foreman. As we passed them, I nodded and spoke, and pretty soon, they were speaking to me.

Three or four workers on the demolition crew were carrying doors and windows to the breezeway and stacking them there. A couple of others loaded them onto a Bobcat and drove them to two Dumpsters, one brown, one black, planted on the grounds next to ours. A pair of men with sledgehammers broke the glass from the doors and windows and hurled it into the black Dumpster. A couple more carried the glassless steel frames to the brown Dumpster. Both the glass and the steel, I was happy to see, were being recycled.

Two or three of the demolition crew were Hondurans, but the others, more than a dozen, said they were from El Salvador. One of the Salvadorans was a skinny young man with protruding teeth. We began exchanging quips each time I came to the truck. After Sung and Jack and I had unloaded it, he sat with us on afternoon break.

The young man lost no time in telling me that he liked Americans. When the 2001 Salvadoran earthquake had hit, he said, Americans had rebuilt his neighborhood and even his church. Volunteers flew to San Salvador from churches across the United States, he told me.

He said that he was twenty-six, that he'd been in the United States only two weeks, and that though he had brothers who had been in town for nearly twenty years, he'd had to leave a wife and two children behind.

I asked how he'd gotten permission to work.

"Oh, I came illegally," he confessed in an unworried way.

"Well, where did you buy the papers that allowed you to work?" I asked, mentioning that I'd once bought a fake residency permit, or green card, myself.

"To be honest," he said, "I am here on this job because the Lord makes a way. Look at me," he continued. "The Holy Spirit told me to come to the United States for two years. He said that I'd get a blessing if I did. Well, here I am. I got here on a Sunday, and if you can believe this, on Monday morning I had a job. I didn't even have to look. People came to my house to ask if I wanted to work. It was a blessing." He was quite pleased with the job too. "I made two hundred dollars as soon as I had worked twenty-four hours!" he exclaimed.

He didn't know whether his net pay was before or after taxes and Social Security deductions, but in my head I did the math: The Salvadorans were earning more than eight dollars an hour.

The demolition foreman, a mustached older man, was passing by, and hearing money mentioned, he stopped to listen.

"Well, how much are you guys making?" he asked me a little briskly.

"Six seventy-five an hour," I told him in Spanish.

"You should get a regular job!" he snorted.

By the time the younger Salvadoran and I had finished our chat, three o'clock was near. The man with the stubbly beard, whom we by now regarded as our straw boss, came over and told us that we could go home.

On our drive back to the Labor-4-U hall, Sung stopped at a convenience store as he usually did, after cruising past several, scanning their signs to save a penny or two per gallon on gasoline: no brand loyalty, as with cigarettes. He'd add five or ten dollars' worth of gasoline to his tank, but never fill it. He had never filled the tank, he told me, because Jeep Cherokees have twenty-gallon tanks. Filling it would have cost him a day's wage.

Dolly sent Sung, Jack, and me back to the schoolyard job the next morning. The place was humdrum until about ten, when a crowd of demolition men and other workers gathered around a portico of one the classroom buildings, as if watching a fight. I joined them.

The portico was about sixteen by twelve feet, with a ceiling of four four-by-eight plywood sheets, hung about ten feet aboveground. Screws held the plywood sheets to a lattice-like steel framework, which couldn't be seen. Steel straps, about two feet long, were also hidden above the plywood. They held the framework to the concrete ceiling, twelve or fourteen feet above the ground.

The demolition men had been attempting to bring down the ceiling assembly, but when they pried with crowbars, the plywood gave way on only one edge. A short Honduran had decided that the only remedy was to go into the narrow opening they'd made with the crowbars.

He crawled into the darkness above the ceiling, carrying a bolt cutter, a supersized tin snip. Within a few seconds, those of us on the ground began to hear snaps; he was cutting the steel hangers. Each time he cut two or three hangers, the ceiling would drop, maybe an inch, maybe two. He kept cutting, but the ceiling no longer dropped when he snipped. Something was making it stick in place.

The men in the crowd hung their heads, unsure what their comrade should do. A couple of minutes passed. Two or three wiseacres hollered to the man inside that it had been nice knowing him, and that they'd take charge of his widow and his final paycheck.

The ceiling had fallen enough that the Honduran was sitting on it, legs outspread in front of him, back hunched. Now he tried to stand, stomping the plywood as he rose. The ceiling gave way another couple of inches on its free side. He kept stomping and stomping and it dropped some more, perhaps three or four inches.

Then he moved into its center, stomping as he went. The ceiling began to give way on another edge, then a third. We could now see his brogans and the lower part of his jeans. The problem, his heroics had revealed, was that the plywood had apparently expanded; it was wedged against the brick walls and pillars of the portico. He continued stomping until the ceiling was nearly three feet beneath its original location, low enough for other men to begin freeing it with saws. Then he crawled out, to a round of cheers.

Central Americans are not bullfight fans, but had they been, his spectators would have been roaring, *"Olé!"*

I spent a good part of the rest of the morning thinking about what I'd have done had I been in his shoes. I'd have insisted that we start with a screwdriver and dismantle the ceiling, panel by panel. That would have taken two men at least half an hour. Then I would have cut the straps and let the framework fall, a section at a time, another fifteen or twenty minutes. All told, I figured that it would have taken two men at least an hour to safely do the job.

The Honduran had done it in fifteen minutes. Had his valor not drawn a crowd, his gambit would have saved labor time.

By eleven, the three of us had run out of things to do. Jack didn't mind. He disappeared to smoke, and maybe to nap. I sat on a short duct, in plain view of the straw boss and the foreman, both of them standing at one of the battlefield desks. Sung felt useless, so he invented a task, pulling cellophane from the ducts. Doing so made sense, or so it seemed to me: The crewmen had to remove those coverings before they could assemble the ducts.

I sat watching Sung—who was not in view of his superiors—until the stubble-faced man, our straw boss, came to me, advising that I go to a dark corner behind the ducts so that nobody would take note of my idleness. I moved into the corner, but I didn't like my surroundings because my only view was of ducts. So I, too, began removing cellophane wrappings and wadding them, making spheres about the size of softballs.

A few minutes later, the straw boss saw what I was doing and came striding, telling me to desist. The wrapping had to be left in place, he said.

I asked why.

"Well, it's kind of like this," he tried to explain. "You see, everything here, all these ducts, well, inside, they've got to be clean, like this was a hospital."

His explanation made no sense to me, but naturally, I quit.

Then he told me to replace the cellophane wrappers that I'd removed—and he walked off.

It was of course impossible to carry out his order. The cellophane softballs were on the floor and they were dusty now. Undoing the spheres would have taken a long time.

The straw boss hadn't seen Sung, so I slipped over to him and relayed what I'd been told. He paid me no mind. I slunk back to my corner and waited until noon.

At lunch we sat with the straw boss under a tree in the park. In chatting, the three of us learned that he and the other semiskilled men worked for Labor-4-U too. They'd been drawing weekly checks, distributed on Thursdays, for six months to a year. The straw boss didn't cite a dollar amount, but he let us know that he and his buddies were earning wages higher than ours.

But when I made reference to the morning and afternoon dispatchers at Labor-4-U, and to the routine of the hall, the straw boss seemed to know nothing and made no reply. He denied knowing anything about Real Deal too. My impression was that he had been hired by Labor-4-U and the air-conditioning firm on the same day—that in effect, Labor-4-U was fronting workers for companies whose regular employees were covered by medical plans, and who earned vacation pay and the like. The gambit was obvious: In seeking contracts, the air-conditioning company could brag to public officials and other humanitarians that all of its employees—without getting specific—were covered by benefit packages. Even more important, people on Labor-4-U payrolls could be laid off at the end of a job and would be eligible for unemployment benefits only if they quit the agency.

The straw boss said that he was waiting for the air-conditioning company to keep a promise to hire him on a regular status—*de planta*, as Mexicans would term it—something that he expected to happen any day.

After lunch, a truck arrived with more ducts. We unloaded them and put them in rough order, according to their approximate sizes. Pretty soon Walter called us to his desk. He wanted us to find certain ducts and carry them to another part of the building, where assembly was under way. He described the ducts by size.

On a breezeway outside, a Bobcat with a jackhammer attached to its front end had been pulverizing a concrete patio. The air was thick with concrete dust, which had settled onto the cellophane that covered the tops of the ducts. The stickers that bore the sizes of the ducts were on their inside surfaces. We couldn't see through the dust-laden cellophane to read their numbers. I tried to brush it away with my gloves, but that didn't work. Static electricity, I suppose, held the dust in place.

We were unable to tell at a glance exactly what size a duct might be, whether, for example, a duct was fourteen or sixteen inches wide. Noticing our confusion, Walter gave Jack a tape measure, but none was available for me or Sung.

Among the stickers pasted onto every duct was one bearing a unique number like 1093 or 1094, 2521 or 2526. Walter's blueprints noted ducts only by size, but he also had a list in which each duct was categorized by type and size—and by its unique number. He told us to find the ducts using those numbers.

But the unique numbers were on stickers inside the ducts too. Sung began removing cellophane again, this time so that he could read the stickers. Jack was soon doing the same. I decided to be a bit more careful. I rammed my fingers into the cellophane, creating holes about three inches long and two inches wide, big enough to allow me to peer inside. The only problem was that to locate a duct that Walter wanted, sometimes I had to punch holes in a half-dozen others.

We located and moved all of the ducts that Walter told us to get, and then we unloaded another truck. At afternoon break on the parking lot, we were lolling about, wondering if anything remained to be done, when Walter appeared, plainly irritated. He sent Jack and me to his pickup truck to find a roll of cellophane nearly three feet wide, and sent Sung into one of the buildings for a roll of duct tape. Then he told us to replace the cellophane on the ducts.

Jack carried a box cutter, me, a pocketknife. Somebody loaned Sung a blade of some kind. Each of us worked by ourselves from the common rolls of cellophane and tape. Sung, I noticed, was pulling whole swathes from the roll, completely wrapping the uncovered ducts, head to foot. Jack and I cut smaller pieces, rewrapping only the tops of the ducts.

It was slow work, not made any easier by the dust that the Bobcat kept throwing into the air. Some of the pieces were already so dusty that the duct tape wouldn't stick to their sides.

A few minutes before quitting time, Walter and the straw boss came by. They were sneering. The straw boss picked up the roll of cellophane. Then he stretched a length of it over the top of a whole row of ducts. Walter cut the cellophane for him. They moved to another row, then another. Instead of rewrapping one duct at a time, they were covering half a dozen ducts in a sweep.

When they finished, Walter signed our ticket and told us that we could leave, though it was yet a bit early. Both he and the straw boss were miffed. I didn't much care because at the end of every day of labor, I was exhausted. Only the vision of a shower and sleep made a difference to me.

When the three of us arrived at the Labor-4-U hall, we formed a line with workers returning from other jobs, turning in tickets.

"I've got a call for a night job, cleanup, food court at a mall. The job starts at nine," the dispatcher hollered.

A burst of white went past my eye. It was Sung, rushing to claim the job.

As he brushed past me on his way out, I stopped him.

"How long do you reckon that night job will last?" I asked.

"I hope it lasts all night," he said. "If I can get me a couple of hours of sleep before nine, I've got it made!"

Sung may have been as clueless as Jack and me, but for him, any ticket was the start of a lucky day.

COLLEGE BOYS

Sometimes a workingman can't do what he's asked, and sometimes he's a fool to try: That's the conclusion I drew one Tuesday after reporting to work for a crew from the generation that will lead, guide, or manage the nation's future.

Four of us from Labor-4-U arrived about half an hour before starting time, 7:45, at a job site just blocks from the labor hall, on the wooded grounds of a nearby university. Its proximity meant that we'd have no fares to pay. The job description Dolly gave us, "unloading a truck," sounded promising too.

It was the kind of job, I figured, whose crew would ordinarily include Real Deal and a couple of his acolytes, but he hadn't been at the hall. Maybe he was in jail again, somebody said.

Since we were early, we found spots to sit and to recline. I struck up a conversation, first, with one of the two fortyish men on our crew, a lanky, pockmarked black named Lamar. For more than two years, he said, he'd been working a weekly ticket on a garbage crew. He'd started at six dollars an hour and had been promoted to an eight-dollar rate when he took on a tougher route, with more cans to lift.

The job had been lucrative, as far as Lamar was concerned, because it usually required fifty, sometimes sixty, hours per week. He had made $25,000 during the previous year, he said contentedly. But the trash-collecting company had decided not to renew its contract with Labor-4-U, and as an employee of a day-labor agency, he was not entitled to jobless benefits. Now he was working with the likes of me.

Also on the crew was Jamal, a young man in his late twenties or early thirties whom I knew from Automax outings. He was one of the hot-rodders, when his hands weren't fiddling with his hair. He wore it in a style of thousands of twists, or ties, which he reviewed or revised constantly. It was a nervous habit, I suppose—better than smoking anyway.

A third member of the crew was a husky white in his forties. The ticket was his first at the labor hall. The day before, he told me, he'd been working as a volunteer at a charity thrift shop, discharging a community-service sentence for driving while intoxicated.

About 8:15 a cream-colored rental van drove by, followed by an 18-wheeler, slowly and cautiously navigating down the narrow campus street. We followed the truck.

The van parked. Six young men piled out. They were fresh-faced and tousle-headed. Five were white, one black. One of the whites wore a gray T-shirt whose back bore the legend "Supervisor." The other T-shirts said "Installer." It was summertime. They wore short pants.

We greeted them, but they merely nodded. They didn't have time to bother with us yet. The 18-wheeler was backing into an even narrower street, lined by cars, parallel-parked on one side. The boys waved and whistled for fifteen minutes while the trucker wrestled with his rig. Its long trailer was a tight fit.

The driver was easing into place in front of a three-story dormitory whose architecture dated to Depression days. We leaned up against a brick wall that surrounded its concrete stairs. The stairs rose perhaps eight feet above a sidewalk.

Moving furniture into even multistory buildings is ordinarily a breeze. One slides it from the rear of a truck, stacks it onto a dolly, pushes the dolly into an elevator, stops on the appropriate floor, and rolls the dolly into a room. After that, if the furniture is boxed, one cuts it free and slides it into place. Sometimes light assembly work is required, but the hardest part of the task is usually crushing or cutting boxes and carrying the pieces to a truck or a Dumpster.

But Lamar was nervous. He stepped from our wall onto the sidewalk and paced the front side of the venerable red-brick dormitory twice, his eyes fixed on its roofline. Then he came to the spot where I was leaning and muttered, "This place doesn't have an elevator."

I couldn't believe him, so I stepped to the curb where the college boys were whistling and waving, guiding the truck. I asked the young man in the Supervisor shirt about the elevator. Barely turning his head toward me, he said that building didn't have one.

I turned toward Lamar, who pointed straight at me.

"I am looking at the elevator!" he quipped.

Alarmed, everyone started peppering the young men with questions. As each responded, we pieced together a picture of their—and our—circumstances. They worked for an out-of-town installation company, a firm that equips office buildings, military bases, hotels, and in summer months, college dormitories. For summer work on campuses, their company hired college students, paying them ten to twelve dollars an hour, plus lodging costs and a per diem fee for meals. The youngsters came from a university a thousand miles away. They were spending the summer, they said, on a working tour of far-flung college towns and bars. Our assumption, I believe, was that we would assist or perhaps team with them.

Once the truck was in place, we helped the six young men pull dollies out of the rear of its trailer, which was otherwise filled with maple-stained chests of drawers about five feet tall, wrapped in filmy Styrofoam. We started to climb inside.

"No, you guys are going to carry this stuff to the third floor," the young supervisor said.

We bunched together and followed him indoors. The stairways were perhaps five feet wide. Two flights led to each floor, each flight separated by a landing perhaps eight feet square. The landings were covered with venerable terrazzo.

My right knee complained as I climbed the stairs, but worse, at each landing I started to pant.

"Now, I want you to work two men to a chest," the supervisor said.

He opened a door to one of the rooms—all of which were uninhab-ited—and showed us where to place our cargoes. Then we followed him downstairs. His comrades had loaded several chests onto dollies and pushed them to the base of the concrete stairs. The rest was up to us.

When I later checked the installation company's Web site, I saw a picture of two rosy-cheeked collegians guiding a chest of drawers across a stairwell. But the supervisory boy had made it clear: Things weren't going to be picture-perfect on this job.

Someone asked the supervisor who had carried furniture up to the first two floors.

"Oh, we did that yesterday with a crew of gofers," he said.

None of us knew what he meant: Were workers from competing labor halls mere gofers? We also wondered what had happened to those guys.

It was clear to me that the job would take six to eight hours, and that even if my knee could withstand the ascents, my lungs wouldn't hold. I told one of the college boys that I had a bad knee, and asked if I couldn't work on the ground, helping to lower the chests from the truck. He motioned me to the supervisor, who said that he and his crew would take care of that task.

He was polite, but I was peeved. Six men, young and hale, were getting the easy work, while the tough chore went to a lesser number of the older and infirm.

If I refused the ticket, I didn't know if I'd ever be hired at the hall again, but it didn't make any difference: I couldn't do the job. I went back to the hall and explained to Stella and Dolly that my knee wouldn't handle the job; I didn't mention my lungs. Dolly said that she understood my circumstances because she sometimes suffered from spinal arthritis. But by then, no other ticket was available to me.

The guy who volunteered to take my place was wearing a black T-shirt bearing the legend "Beware of the Educated Black Man." The T-shirt, he told me, was a gift from a sister of his, a young woman who was enrolled in an institution that cultivates the sense of privilege that we confronted that day.

Wednesday morning I looked in the hall for those who'd been sent to the job with me. None of them appeared. Dolly dispatched a fresh crew.

On Thursday, Lamar turned up. He said that on the day that I'd left, the crew had unloaded for more than seven hours and that he'd been unable to repeat—to tote bedsteads up the stairs—because his back was sore. On Friday one or two of the others drifted in. All gave reports of a similar kind. A single shift at the dormitory job—one payday—imposed upon its laborers what was, in effect, a one-day layoff. The whole bunch of us, temporary workers, had been expendable as well.

Life is not always an elevator for college kids, I knew. But apparently, some of them can rest assured that if they must for a season make themselves available to labor, inferiors will scale any stairs that fate might place in their path.

12

The Dead Man Job:
A Soap Opera in Four Acts

That afternoon I was back at the hall, having finished a turn on an Automax ticket. I had accepted the ticket after Stella, the hall's manager, had forbidden me to go to a job that paid better, and on which I knew my work was appreciated.

Stella and Jason, the afternoon dispatcher, were behind the counter when I came in.

"Since I've put in my day for Labor-4-U, can I go by that other job?" I asked. They already knew what job I was talking about.

They looked at each other for a moment.

"Well, since we don't have a deal with them anymore, I guess you can do that," Jason grunted.

I skipped out of the hall before they could change their minds. Trudging toward the job site, which wasn't more than a half-mile away, I asked myself why I wanted to go back.

The task, sorting through the papers of a dead man, had been a hassle to start, but had been easy to perform, and the pay, at $7.25 an hour, had been better than average. Our bosses had been considerate, perhaps even to a fault.

But what compelled me to return wasn't only that. I wanted to go back, it dawned on me, not because I wanted to work, but because I felt

a sense of obligation—and also, I'm afraid, because I was getting wise.
I was cruising for a tip.

The job had started a couple of days after I'd turned down the dormitory assignment. I'd spent two days without a ticket, waiting, and
worrying that I'd been put on the B-team again. The third of those
mornings, a Friday, prospects had looked bleak. I had watched as Dolly
dispatched three dozen people to work, including Jack Clemmons, the
cracker who moved at least as slowly as me.

To abate anxiety, I had weeks before set a time beyond which I
wouldn't wait for a ticket. That Friday morning I'd let my usual seven-
thirty deadline pass. An hour and twenty minutes later, Stella called me
to the counter.

"You're on standby, so don't leave. And you'll probably have to
work tomorrow," she muttered.

As I was returning to my chair, a black worker with low-hanging
pants who I knew as Leroy came rushing up to me, asking what time
I had signed in. When I told him, he darted to the counter and began
wrangling with Stella, I assume on the grounds that she was obligated
to assign work on a first-come, first-served basis. That wasn't true: A
sign on the wall behind her said that the hall matched jobs with skills,
not sign-in times.

Stella ignored him and called two other guys, telling them that they
were on standby with me.

When, an hour later, no clients had shown, we three gathered on
the hall's porch to sift the situation. Jimmy, the guy from the culvert
and truck-unloading jobs, who had also been waiting for work, was
already outside. Loudmouthed Leroy quickly appeared.

One of those assigned to standby with me was a black man in his
fifties, Alton, and the other was a fortyish guy I knew as Raymond, a
round-shouldered, pudgy, coffee-colored warehouse worker who came
to the labor hall two or three mornings a week.

Raymond, who claimed more than two years of experience at the
hall, took the lead in our conversation. His manner was almost pater-
nal, and the others acceded, as if he were a man in the know. His take
was that though they'd told him something about "driving a truck,"

"unloading," and "keeping track of paperwork," the dispatchers didn't really know how many of us would be needed, what our task would be, or when our clients would show.

Jimmy and Leroy nevertheless clamored to be included on the job, as if Raymond could decide who would get the ticket.

In his desperation, Leroy even accosted me, his nose nearly touching mine.

"You ain't been working here long, have you? I ain't seen you around," he said before I could answer.

Jimmy wanted to join us, but Raymond doused his hopes because Jimmy admitted that on two different tickets, he'd already logged thirty-five hours for the week.

"Man, you should go home," Raymond scolded. "You know that they're not going to send you out today."

That, no doubt, was true. Laws governing overtime deprive workers of jobs at the end of every week. If a worker logs more than forty hours for a client company, it, and not the labor hall, is liable for time-and-a-half overtime pay. But if he or she works, for example, thirty hours for one client and fourteen for another, the labor hall must pay the differential. Temporary-labor services avoid that expense by ignoring workers who report after they near the forty-hour threshold.

Raymond questioned Leroy about his hours. He had clocked thirty-one, he said—enough to put him in the danger zone—but he insisted that three of those hours shouldn't be counted. He'd spent them, he said, doing mopping and mowing at the hall, on the Labor-4-U payroll.

"Brother, you know how those people are," Raymond said, dismissing Leroy's appeal too.

Jimmy drifted away, leaving the three of us alone with Leroy. About ten thirty, Alton went inside, only to learn from Dolly that he'd been cut from the ticket because the clients had telephoned to say that they no longer needed a driver: Two men would do, one to unload and one to process paperwork. Alton wasn't dismayed, because like Raymond, he'd already been out on a ninety-minute unloading job, for which he'd been paid for four hours.

But nothing assuaged Leroy. He was insistent when, a few minutes later, Dolly and Stella came outside for a cigarette break. He began badgering them about the ticket. Dolly said that she'd picked me for the paperwork job because I had a bad knee and hadn't worked for days. Still complaining that I was being favored, Leroy slunk away.

About eleven, our clients—two young white women—arrived at the hall in a compact car that I took to be a rental vehicle. One of them, who introduced herself as Lourdes, was of a stocky build and in her early twenties, with straight brown hair that fell to the middle of her back. The other, a blonde named Alicia, appeared to be in her early thirties, though she later told me that she was forty-one. Both had black backpacks strapped to their shoulders, and the younger woman's back-pack carried an embroidery patch that showed a tiger beneath several Chinese characters. These kids are students, I told myself.

The two went inside with Stella and Dolly. I slipped in behind them, trying to hear what was said at the counter. I saw one of them pass a credit card to Stella or Dolly, and thought I heard Stella or Dolly tell the clients to write a check for $78. The procedure was a bit irregu-lar—the labor hall usually bills its clients or takes credit card numbers by telephone—and it was clear that the pair were not regular custom-ers. It struck me as odd, too, that Dolly gave our ticket to them, not Raymond or me.

Outside, the pair described the job. Their father, Greg Curtis, had dropped dead in his apartment some four or five days earlier. We had to clean the place. Raymond was quick to express condolences, but the two women only smiled, as if what he said was beside the point.

Her father had been a "hoarder," one of the two warned us, adding that his eccentricity was a symptom of a mental disorder.

I asked how old he had been. One of them said that he had been fifty-eight, but the other claimed that he'd been born in 1939. Their imprecision—a ten-year discrepancy—one of them explained, was the result of their father's marriages and divorces: The two women were half-sisters, and the younger of them, Lourdes—who told me that she was a student at an Ivy League college—had only briefly lived with her dad. They had come to town, they explained, to settle his affairs.

We followed the sisters to the job site in Raymond's aging white Cadillac. The red-brick apartment complex where Curtis had lived had been built to house World War II beneficiaries of the GI Bill. In subsequent years, its dozen L-shaped, three-story buildings had attracted tenants who were mostly childless office workers or retirees. Its apartments were air-conditioned by dated window units.

A flatbed truck with wooden railings was parked on the lawn outside the apartment. Its driver, a lanky, fiftyish black man, was standing by.

The ground-floor apartment that Curtis had occupied was in the foot of an L, not its spine. Its door was of heavy wood, painted brown. Curtis had tacked a note to it, telling exterminators to stay out. To the right and left of the door, on the landing of a three- or four-step stairwell, a half-dozen filmy green trash bags were waiting to be carried away, along with a half-dozen kraft grocery-store bags stuffed with old newspapers, plus a couple of boxes of handwritten documents and photos.

The truck driver would take the green bags to a landfill and take the kraft bags to a recycling center, the women said. They planned to put the boxes of papers into storage for review later, one of them explained.

The door opened to an entry room, perhaps ten feet square. To its right was a short hallway whose right wall opened onto a narrow kitchen. A few steps farther down, the hallway opened, on the left, onto an office with multi-pane windows along two of its sides. At the end of the short hallway sat a cavernous bedroom, about eighteen feet by twelve feet, with high ceilings and, like the office, two walls of windows.

The whole place was stacked, nearly floor to ceiling, with browning cardboard boxes containing legal-sized file folders.

The bedroom was so packed that we couldn't figure out where Curtis had slept. The kitchen sink was filled with boxes, which were stacked on the counters too. A narrow passageway led into the bathroom, whose shower-tub unit seemed to be dusty, as if boxes had been stored there as well. Shelves on two sides of the entry room held odds and ends of apparently useless materials, including one of those signs that pizza deliverymen put atop their cars, complete with lights, wiring, and suction cups.

Here and there in the apartment drawers stood open. One was chock-full of plastic dispensers that looked like real lemons.

From their car the sisters brought a bag of yellow rubber gloves, a half-dozen spray cans of Lysol, and two gallons of drinking water.

Our first job was to clear the entry room. Some of its shelves were of plastic, as elsewhere in the apartment, but as his hoard grew, Curtis had apparently run into financial problems. More than half of the shelves in every room were mere planks—or doors!—supported on their ends by document-filled cardboard boxes. He'd even made a few shelves by gluing tubes from rolls of paper towels to the corners of cardboard box tops.

The dead man had unwittingly made our job easier by saving dozens of grocery-store paper bags, some with handles or paper straps. Raymond and I each took an empty box, for handwritten documents and photos, and a paper bag, for the publications and other mass-produced paper items that we were to discard for recycling. We started riffling. At the base of many of the boxes we found dead silverfish, but no roaches.

Raymond apparently wasn't used to making decisions, and the job perplexed him a bit. Our clients had told us to save not only handwritten items and photos, but anything with the dead man's name on it, an instruction that I ignored as soon as I encountered junk mail and telephone bills that dated to 1992. After perhaps forty-five minutes of sorting and stacking, Raymond, still fretting about what to keep and what to toss, volunteered to carry our haul to the truck outside. When that was done, momentarily at a loss, he made three or four calls on his cell phone. The sisters didn't notice, because they were sorting in the bedroom, and with me standing in the entry room, couldn't squeeze by to check on him.

The two women had told us that their father had been trained as an architect, but made his living in "marketing." He had evidently operated a shoestring ad agency from his home.

That explained the second-rate and one-shot publications that I found in the boxes—real estate guides and publications with titles like "Parade of Homes." But it took me a while to discern why I turned up box after box of restaurant menus: Curtis, it appeared, had designed them.

Mixed with the publications were copies of proposal letters to prospective clients and boilerplate missives from them, expressing appreciation for his interest. Several boxes contained tour brochures from the Caribbean, usually in their mailing envelopes. I took it that Curtis had not been traveling, but had instead been collecting ideas for promotion to chambers of commerce. In two or three boxes I found materials he had written to persuade a city council to alter its water tower to resemble a pink flamingo.

At some point, he'd apparently had a staff, or tried to build one. A flyer entitled "Can You?" read:

Can you make money 24/7 worldwide?
Can you make as much money as you want, or are you limited by hourly wage or salary?
Can you make money lying in bed, while taking a nap?

At its bottom, the flyer instructed prospective employees to call his telephone number.

The photos I found were mostly from business expositions, conventions, and the like. I did not find any family photos until I ran into a box that contained nothing else. All of them were framed. It would seem, as his collection of documents rose toward the ceilings, he had run out of space to display them.

Curtis had been a serial hoarder. Many of the documents I found were duplicates of those placed in other files. It appeared that when he thought he had a marketable idea, he'd photocopy his materials to remind himself to sell the idea to a new client. As if it were especially precious, sometimes he would slip a document between clear vinyl covers. Most these were mere magazine ads, as if he had found something admirable in them.

Much of his correspondence was held together with pastel-colored paper clips. He also used clips to mark magazine pages that inspired him. Because the women had been specific about sorting paper and cardboard for recycling—a sign, I thought, of upper-middle-class status—I threw the clips into empty plastic containers.

An hour or two after we'd begun, a portly, graying white man in a white tennis shirt and khaki pants appeared. He introduced himself as Steve Curtis, and in a jovial, rather than mournful, way, explained that he was the dead man's brother. Paging through the boxes of papers that Raymond and I had saved, he was able to make sense of our findings, though he was often amused. Thinking it might be valuable, I had, for example, laid aside a $100,000 stock certificate printed in green on parchment-like paper. It was for a company strangely named the Motor Talent Agency.

"This was for a company he started," Steve said with a chuckle, as if the dead man had christened dozens of oddly named schemes.

I later found a letter that Steve had signed—as an attorney for the dead man in a contractual dispute.

Early in the afternoon Steve left the place and to our pleasure and surprise, came back, half an hour later, with hamburgers and sodas for Raymond and me. I didn't see what he brought for the sisters, but I heard one of them say, "I don't eat meat"—another indicator, as far as I was concerned, of education and wealth.

About four, Uncle Steve left again. By the time he returned, half an hour later, Raymond and I had cleared the entry room and were working in the kitchen. The uncle stepped in and said, "All right, boys, I've got your pay, twenty dollars an hour for six hours, plus a little something extra."

Saying that he'd like us to return on Saturday, he handed each of us seven $20 bills.

We nodded in appreciation—but we were dumbfounded by the sight of cash.

Soon we were outdoors, helping the driver load bags of "paper recyclables," as Lourdes called them. Raymond and I took the opportunity to huddle at a picnic table on the lawn.

"Man, what was that guy doing? Why was he paying us so much?" I asked.

"I don't know, but don't say nothing," Raymond warned me.

"What about the ticket? What if they don't give it to us?" I countered.

It didn't seem likely to me that Steve would tip us $20 an hour on a ticket that paid $7.25 an hour. He was trying to hire us off the books, I reasoned. The problem that I foresaw was that the tickets were numbered. Labor-4-U would want our ticket for bookkeeping purposes and if we didn't turn it in, someone would call us to account.

"Don't go back to the hall today, and don't say nothing to nobody. Just pretend it didn't happen," Raymond advised me.

"Won't they know? Don't they have a copy of the ticket?" I argued.

"They keep a pink copy," Raymond confessed. "But don't worry about it. They ain't going to worry about it. They ain't lost nothing by it. I won't be in on Monday, because of my other job," he continued, "and if I was you, I wouldn't go in on Monday either. Just go in Tuesday and get your repeat on the Automax ticket and don't say anything. Dolly and them will have forgotten about it by then."

It is common on unloading jobs, for example, for day laborers to work half a day on a ticket signed for four hours, but to stay on the job longer, working off the books for nine or ten dollars an hour. Both the client and the workers benefit from that practice. But in such cases the workers return to the hall with a ticket in hand. The paperwork is clear, even if it isn't honest and everybody knows as much.

But openly working off the books was a serious offense, I'd learned a few weeks before when I'd seen Carrie and another woman escorting a man named Theo across the parking lot by his arms. Only seconds before, Stella had told Theo, a fiftyish Greek immigrant who spoke with an accent, that she was suspending him for thirty days. He'd stomped out of the hall shouting hoarse words that I couldn't make out. Even as the women tugged him away he was looking back and cursing.

Early the day before, Dolly had assigned Theo to a ticket. He'd been outside, waiting for a driver to show, when a contractor drove up and offered him a one-day job at ten dollars an hour, off the books. Theo got in the man's pickup and the two drove away. Dolly had to recruit a last-minute replacement and redo the ticket.

I reminded Raymond of the incident, but he didn't think it relevant.

"Dolly might even have been in on this ticket," he speculated. "She might know what's going on. She might have given it to us so that we could make good. If they like you," he added, "Dolly and Stella can do stuff like that. The only thing is, you can't be giving them a hard time like Leroy was doing this morning. If you do that, you don't work."

"Okay," I told him. "I ain't saying nothing."

We loaded the truck and worked until about sundown before begging off. Raymond drove me to the nearest thoroughfare and told me that since I wasn't going to the hall, he wouldn't charge me the usual fare. En route, he continued his rap about the need to keep mum.

As I was walking the three or four blocks back to the spot where I had parked and locked my bicycle—out of sight from the labor hall—a young black man in casual slacks and an apparently brand-new Obama T-shirt came riding past me on the sidewalk. He stopped, only feet away, reached into his pocket, and hailed me.

"I'll bet you could use some change!" he said.

He handed me a dozen coins that I eyeballed as between one and two dollars. It seemed to me that nothing good would come of telling him that I wasn't who I seemed to be. But I wanted him to know that I shared his presidential choice.

"I helped the Obama campaign during the primary," I muttered.

Perhaps he couldn't fathom that an old white man with a George Bush accent had registered voters for Obama.

"Oh, I see, are you a veteran?" he asked.

I told him I wasn't, turned, and walked on.

Given my age and my manual-work attire, he had no reason to suspect that I might be a professor. Instead, he mistook me for a homeless man, and probably a Vietnam vet. So long had I been living and working in disguise, I suppose, that even I had accepted that image as myself.

The problem of the missing ticket still had me worried. By the time I reached my house, perhaps twenty minutes later, I was in a panic.

The situation was rife with danger, as far as I could see. Even if the sisters didn't return the ticket, Labor-4-U would bill their credit card, I feared. If they did turn in the ticket but refused to pay the hourly rate, the company would learn that we'd been working off the books. Not only would Raymond and I be quizzed, but I figured that Dolly would be called on the carpet for having given the ticket to the sisters, not us.

Beyond that, I was a bit troubled by the rate they'd paid us. It was half again as much, from what I knew, as clients ordinarily pay.

Raymond's insistence that we keep mum was too smart by half, I figured, and the only way out was to talk to the sisters. Maybe they'd comprehend my circumstances and agree to a plan for putting the problem to rest.

That afternoon we had carried two old computers and a television to the lawn. Alicia had told me that I could have them if I wanted. They were useless, but I decided to use the TV as an excuse to return, figuring that if the truck driver was still there, I'd just pick up the TV and go without saying anything. Since my bicycle couldn't carry it, I got in my car—a 1974 Volkswagen Beetle.

When I arrived at the parking lot, Alicia and Lourdes were about to drive away. Alicia was at the wheel of their rented compact, Lourdes on the passenger side. Seeing me, Lourdes rolled down her window.

"We like your car," Alicia hollered.

I was again reminded that these sisters had money. The guys at the labor hall would have snorted had they seen my ride.

I walked up to the open window and told the two, "Raymond warned me not to say anything, but I got the impression that y'all didn't know that you're not supposed to pay us in cash."

They said they hadn't known.

"She told us that it would cost twenty dollars an hour, so that's what we paid you," Alicia mumbled.

I informed them that nobody at Labor-4-U had ever earned as much as twenty dollars an hour, and that, in any case, we had to return the ticket to the hall.

Lourdes pulled it out of her backpack and scanned its lines, one of which, she showed me, carried a warning: "Do Not Give Cash to Our Workers." Then she passed it to Alicia.

"Well, what should we do now?" Alicia asked. "Do you plan to give us back the money?"

I told her that I didn't think the idea would work.

"My interest," I explained, "is in staying out of trouble with Raymond, and with the hall too. If I get in trouble with the hall, I may not work again. If I get in trouble with Raymond," I said—counting on the myth of the tough-guy day laborer—"I may not walk again. There are some pretty rough guys working there, you know."

"Maybe we could just not pay you tomorrow," she said, politely searching for common ground.

"I don't think that will fly either," I opined. "Raymond is expecting twenty dollars an hour."

"What kind of thug is he?" she shot back.

"It's not that," I said. "I think he just saw all of this money falling out of the sky and it kind of got to his head. He didn't want to work Saturday, but the money changed his mind."

I proposed that we hold on to the ticket until the job was done, then write that we had worked only four hours that Friday, plus four more on Saturday.

"That way, you'll still be out something, but not as much," I argued.

Both of them agreed. Lourdes came up with a pen and filled in the blanks. I showed her where to sign. But she kept the ticket. I loaded the TV into the car and went home to estimate their losses, for which I felt partly to blame.

My figures showed that if they kept the deal we'd made, they would wind up paying some $600 for our services, about $200 more than they owed. People in the educated classes are often generous, I knew—but still, I went to bed uneasy.

When I awoke in the morning, I went back to my notepad to determine whether I could cover their loss without tipping Raymond to the scheme. If I returned the $140 that they had paid me, and they gave us $20 an hour for our Saturday work, they'd still be short $60 or more.

Raymond had already told me that he couldn't work on Sunday, and that gave me a new idea. If I could secretly return my $140 and could work, off the books and unpaid, for three hours on Sunday, everything would turn out fine. It was a middle-class solution—"Honesty is the best policy," Benjamin Franklin said—and I set out for work early, hoping to catch the two before Raymond came. I reached the apartment at seven thirty, half an hour before the appointed time, took a seat at the picnic table, and waited.

Raymond hadn't arrived by eight, when the two clients appeared on the lawn. I called them over and proposed my scheme.

"No, that's not what we're going to do," Alicia told me coldly. "We're going to give you this ticket at the end of the day, and that's it. We're forgetting about yesterday."

I was puzzled. Was she saying that we'd be governed by my proposal of the afternoon before, or was something else in the air? Had the two stopped by the hall on their way to the apartment and told everything to the dispatchers? Alicia told me to wait outside for Raymond, but after ten minutes, I went into the apartment and started sorting papers again. When Raymond arrived, about fifteen minutes later, the sisters said nothing untoward. At the mid-morning break, Alicia even went out for soft drinks.

The truck driver and an assistant showed up at about eleven. They carried boxes to the stairwell, sat down with the rest of us, and began sorting papers, ostensibly for the first time. These two, I figured, were either reinforcements or our replacements. I scanned the apartment. Much of the office, the bedroom, and the bath were still to be done. If the trucker and his buddy had worked the night before, it hadn't been for long.

Trying to get an idea of the size of the job that lay ahead, I asked Alicia when she and Lourdes planned to return home.

"Well, we both have plane tickets for tomorrow," she said, "but we will probably stay until we get this finished."

About noon, the sisters, Raymond, and I were working in the bedroom. Raymond said that we had to call it a day. Lourdes walked past me on her way outdoors and Raymond followed. I jumped into the line. As we passed through the hallway, I noticed a bulletin board that I didn't think had been hanging there the day before. It bore a message that discomforted me.

Curtis, our paper-shuffling had shown, was a proliferator of catchy small-business slogans like "Commitment is what transforms a promise into reality" and "Those who snooze, lose. Those who sleep, weep." He made copies of these adages and stuck them in file after file. One of these slogans, printed on the dead man's letterhead, was pinned to the cork bulletin board that now hung in the hallway. "Stick to your agreement, go to work and get the job done!" it said.

I wasn't sure how to interpret the slogan, but it seemed likely that the women had posted it the night before.

At the stairwell, Lourdes turned to face us, ticket in hand. She handed it to me and blurted, "Okay, we are square now. Thanks for coming!"

The ticket seemed new and unwrinkled. I passed it to Raymond. We told Lourdes thanks, and left. On the lawn Raymond glanced at the ticket, but didn't tell me what it said.

"They didn't give us money today," I remarked.

"Yeah, but that's okay," he said. "I ain't against money, but I'm not greedy either."

Because Labor-4-U closed for lunch on Saturdays, Raymond told me to meet him there a little before five.

I showed up about four thirty. Raymond's white Caddy was in the parking lot, but he was inside, standing at the counter. I saw him waving his arms at Dolly. I went in and stood behind him.

"You know, that truck driver was telling me that he was getting five hundred dollars for two days," he was saying. "And, man, that place was filthy! It was a health hazard, I'm telling you!"

"I am quite sure that you guys deserved everything you got," Dolly said.

"You can sure say that!" Raymond continued.

"Well, those girls called me, and I had to admit that I hadn't told them not to pay you," Dolly continued. "Just don't say anything about this. If Stella was to find out, I'd be in hot water."

Dolly paid us for four hours, for Saturday only. I said nothing, but was left wondering what the real story had been. What had the sisters told Dolly? How did they get her to agree to forget Friday's ticket? Had Raymond and Dolly conspired about what to say in my presence? Maybe Dolly's calm demeanor was an act to cover up a plot, formed with Raymond, that Dolly intended to benefit me as well. My guess was that whatever had happened, I would go down as a dullard who couldn't be trusted.

Early Monday morning I was standing on the porch when Dolly and Stella came out for a smoke break. Though they stood fifteen feet away, it was easy to overhear them. The sisters had telephoned the office to ask for workers again, and Dolly was relating the confusion that had arisen over the Friday ticket in a she-said, I-said, he-said way. Stella wasn't sympathetic. She upbraided Dolly for having "blown it off."

I slunk inside, fearing what would come next. When the two of them returned to the counter, Stella called me. Though she was agitated, she told me, "As far as I am concerned, the money those girls gave you was a tip."

I was stunned that she would take our side.

Apparently, the clients had asked for me to be put on the ticket. Raymond wasn't coming in, so Dolly added Tony Silvio, a handsome Italian American kid in his early twenties, who had signed on at the hall about a week earlier.

Tony was a cheerful but somewhat pugnacious and boastful type. One morning he had called attention to his five o'clock shadow. "Italian beards grow fast, see. That's a sign of being macho," he'd said.

He was wearing a pair of jeans that had a rip from a back pocket all the way to his boots. I'd asked him about the tear.

"It's all right. I wear shorts underneath and the only person who is going to look is a faggot and if one of them says anything, I'll lay him out," he bragged.

But Tony had a kinder side too. The dead-man job wasn't set to start until ten, and in the interval Timmy, a white boy who had befriended him, came in.

Timmy was of ordinary height, but rail-thin. Soft-spokenness and pale blue eyes contributed to my image of him as a weak or recessive type. Standing on the porch—I was with them—Timmy complained that the week before, he'd only caught out once. Tony, on the other hand, had worked three days out of the four he'd reported.

Tony apparently didn't know that new workers are usually kept busy until the dispatchers assess their worth; he wasn't lucky, he was new. He felt sorry for Timmy and went inside to talk to the dispatchers. A few minutes later, somebody came to the front door to tell me that Stella wanted me at the counter. She had given me the ticket, and now wanted it back. She handed me a new one, bearing Timmy's name and mine.

"Tony is being generous," she said.

Before going outdoors, I had been sitting in the hall with Wilkins, the ex-convict from the asphalt job. He had heard that the dead-man ticket was a gravy train, and had told me that he'd like to be assigned if Raymond didn't show. When Dolly had picked Tony, I'd apologized. When the switch to Timmy was made, I was worried because I hadn't been to the counter to lobby for Wilkins, and for the second time that day, I had been paired with a white. Wilkins was inflamed.

"Come outside," he snapped at me. I followed him to the porch, not knowing what would ensue.

"Man, I fucked myself!" he exclaimed. "I fucked myself, I fucked myself."

I couldn't fathom what he meant.

"That job was waiting for somebody, and what did I do? I didn't say nothing! I should have told Dolly when you first came in that if they was sending anybody to that job with you, it had to be me!"

Before he could fully decompress, Dolly called me and Timmy inside.

"I'm going to take you to the job," she said.

"We can walk," I told her.

"I know that, but I have to get that Lourdes to sign a ticket for Friday," she explained. "I don't want you to say anything. Let me do the talking."

At the apartment Dolly produced a ticket, presumably for Friday, and two envelopes that she said had to do with insurance. She handed them to Lourdes.

"All right, but if I sign, does this obligate me to pay for Friday? I don't want to sign anything that does that," she said.

Dolly said that she didn't know, but that Stella would call when she decided the paperwork was in order.

I began holding my breath, waiting for the call.

The two sisters had spent Sunday working in the apartment. In its office they had stacked doors on top of boxes to make sorting desks. Green plastic chairs sat at each desk. Lourdes had me raise the doors while she stuck extra boxes beneath each end, making the desks higher for Timmy and me. That was of no help, since I stood no taller than they, but it was nice gesture, anyhow.

I took a seat at the western window, Timmy at the window on the north. Shortly the truck driver came in and sat down facing the windowless eastern wall. As we sorted, we ran into unexpected things, including three sets of soiled underwear—proof, in our minds, that Curtis had been out of his mind. I was also irritated to find that in several boxes, he had substituted unused Priority Mail envelopes for folders, an abuse of public trust, as far as I was concerned.

But we also found in the boxes a few brand-new, cheap toys—jacks, balls, little airplanes—that I took to be commercial samples. Timmy asked us to set them aside for his son.

As he told it, he was twenty-three. He'd dropped out of high school at eighteen because his girlfriend was pregnant with the boy. He and the mother had subsequently divorced, but she allowed him to visit the child on weekends. She had remarried. After a couple of fistfights, Timmy said, he and the stepfather had learned to coexist.

In the years since he'd left school, he confessed, he had compiled a misdemeanor record for drinking and fighting. That explained why, I thought, shy and timid as he seemed, around the hall he was regarded as Real Deal's minion.

He'd also earned a general equivalency diploma, and had tried to join the Marine Corps. Its recruiters told him that before they'd enlist him, he had to complete a few credit hours at a junior college. The problem, Timmy said, was that he needed a car to do that. Working at Labor-4-U was his way of accumulating cash, he claimed. I didn't know whether to believe him or not, because redemption tales are a dime a dozen at labor halls.

In one of the dead man's boxes I found a file about Monica Lewinsky, which I decided to save just because I knew that the sisters would laugh. I also found a photo of Curtis, taken, Alicia guessed, about three years earlier. It showed only his head. He was wearing a black baseball cap and outsized, black-framed eyeglasses. He had a narrow face and grizzly gray stubble, a stunted beard. He was smiling broadly, but nobody knew why.

Uncle Steve came in and joined the sisters, sorting in the bedroom. A few minutes later I ran across the dead man's funeral wishes, a couple of handwritten pages on a yellow legal notepad. I took it to the sisters. They glanced at it and passed it to Steve, who stopped sorting to read its lines. Later he told me that the note's prescriptions couldn't be carried out because it had been written some fifteen years earlier. Curtis had asked for memorial services in two states, but his connections elsewhere were forgotten and cold.

Shortly after lunch—Steve and the sisters brought food again—a cell phone rang. The sisters went outside to take the call. I saw them, minutes later, making a return call of some kind. They were outdoors for more than an hour. I suspected that the flurry of phone calls had to do with the ticket, but it was not my place to ask.

By late afternoon, the trucker, Jimmy, and I had finished the office. We started carrying boxes from the bedroom to the sorting desks. As we unearthed boxes in the bedroom, we found two upholstered armchairs, one stacked atop the other, and a China cabinet that, Steve told us, dated to 1880. We also encountered a wind-up dresser clock that had been given to Curtis on the day of his birth. So buried had it been that we were sure it hadn't been wound in ten years.

At one end of the bedroom we ran into a mattress, stacked beneath levels of boxes and on top of two levels more. It smelled of urine, and some of the boxes were wet. Fortunately, Timmy got the job of clearing the area, not me. The sisters, who had returned indoors, gave him a paper face mask, but he said that it didn't help much.

Before we left, about five thirty, Alicia called me into a corner. Placing a finger across her lips, she handed me a notepad on which she had written a message, asking if I would return the next day at fourteen dollars an hour, without advising Labor-4-U. I motioned her to follow me outside.

I had a repeat ticket, every Tuesday, for the Automax job, I told her. Labor-4-U would be expecting me. I offered to skip the Automax ticket if she'd call Dolly and ask that I be reassigned. She shook her head.

"We're thinking that we'll sue them if nobody refunds our cash and they bill our credit card for Friday," she told me.

Then she asked if I would be willing to return the $140 I'd been paid. I was by then wary of side deals. I'd do whatever Stella told me to do, I said.

We left the matter unresolved.

When Timmy and I reached the hall, we gave our ticket to Jason, who was on duty as afternoon dispatcher.

"I am sick and tired of those girls you are working for, and so is everybody else in the office!" he grumbled. "They've been calling us all day. I say, ignorance is no excuse!"

Not knowing whether he was referring to the clueless sisters or to me, I kept mum.

Just then the telephone rang. It was one of the sisters, saying that she wanted Timmy and me to return in the morning.

Jason told her someone would contact her when morning came. Then he turned to us.

"Both of you can go back if you want," he said, "but the way those girls are, I wouldn't be surprised if Stella canceled the service."

I signed in early that Tuesday, about six. Dolly came in a bit late, about six thirty. A few minutes afterward she called me to the counter and asked if I wanted to repeat on the dead-man job. It paid more than the four-hour Automax ticket, I explained.

"Did Raymond threaten you?" she asked.

I told her that he hadn't.

"Well, I want you to tell that to Stella," she muttered.

I moved down the counter to relate my story.

"Stella, I told those ladies that I had to get along with Labor-4-U and Raymond. I told her that if I made you mad, I might not work again, and that if I made Raymond mad, I might not walk again. But I didn't say that anybody threatened me."

I added that Alicia had said that she would sue if nobody repaid the cash, and that her uncle was a lawyer.

I shouldn't have said that.

"Well, let her go ahead and sue," Stella shouted, loudly enough for the whole hall to hear. "We've got plenty of lawyers, and damn good ones too!"

A few minutes later, Stella called me back to the counter. She didn't admit it, but she had changed her mind. She was no longer maintaining that "the money those girls gave you was a tip," but instead said that I had to repay the cash "or you'll never work here again."

I offered to take the money to the sisters, get a receipt, and bring it back.

"No. You have to pay the money to us," she spat.

"What about Raymond?" I asked.

She said that she was expecting him shortly for the Automax job and that "if he doesn't pay us, he won't work here again either."

I looked around the hall. Everyone was watching us. I reached for my billfold and began slowly counting twenties onto the counter.

"Look at this!" I exclaimed, turning to my peers. "We come to Labor-4-U so that we can get money from them. And here I am, giving money to the hall."

Several guys laughed, but Stella wasn't amused. She put away the money, typed out the paperwork for Friday's ticket, and paid me for six hours at $7.25.

A few minutes afterward I went to the counter again because I didn't know where Stella and Dolly planned to send me. Alicia, I recalled, had said something the day before that made me fear new trouble if I returned. She had said that she would only need me to clean the place, a chore that I didn't think would take much time. I doubted that she knew about the four-hour minimum rule. I asked Dolly to call the sisters and explain that no matter how many hours

I worked, she had to pay for at least four. Dolly said that she'd make the call.

But pretty soon she called the Automax job. Both Timmy's name and mine were on the list.

"I thought we were going to work for those ladies," I said as meekly as I could.

Dolly looked at Stella.

"Just go on to the Automax job. If those girls are talking about suing us, I don't want to do business with them," Stella said.

"Yeah," I argued, "but if we pay back the money, they won't sue, and I've already paid."

"But Raymond isn't here and his cell-phone number doesn't work and I just don't want to deal with them," she told me.

As I neared the apartment after the Automax job, I found myself regretting that my loose tongue had caused problems for all of us twice—once, when I'd spoken to the sisters about the cash payment, and again that morning, when I told Stella that they were threatening to sue. But if I confessed my indiscretions to Raymond, I knew I'd be ostracized, and Stella didn't seem to be a person whom any apology would mollify. That meant that I could make amends only with the sisters, if I found them. I resolved to do so, whether they had work for me, or a tip for me, or not.

It was about two when I got to the grounds. The yard was clean. No trash bags and no boxes of paper were sitting outside. A short U-Haul truck stood near the entry door, loaded with the antique furniture we'd found in the bedroom and with boxes of the documents we'd saved.

Alicia was in the office. By way of apology, I told her that I'd repaid the $140 to the hall. She already knew, it seemed. I told her that Raymond hadn't shown and that Stella hadn't been able to locate him. She knew that too. Obviously, she and Stella had spoken.

The floors needed sweeping, but the office was nearly bare and the other rooms were stripped. I figured that the truck driver, Bill, had come to help that morning.

Alicia said that they had nothing for me to do, but that she wanted to give me a tip. But she spoke very softly. She went into the bedroom, where Uncle Steve and Lourdes were working. I stayed in the office, waiting.

After a few minutes, the uncle stepped outside, maybe to take something to the U-Haul truck. I slipped into the office. Lourdes was sitting on the floor, Alicia kneeling beside her. They were whispering. When I entered, Alicia rose and handed me some cash. I slipped it into my billfold without counting it. I told them thanks for the job and that I was sorry for the friction.

As I was leaving, Steve reappeared. He halted me to say so long and to declare that if the cash from Friday wasn't repaid, he would sue Labor-4-U, me, and Raymond. I apologized for the trouble and told him that I had already squared accounts.

"Well, you tell Raymond that we'll be looking for him," he said.

I shuffled out and stopped at the hall so that Jason would see that I'd not gone back to work for the dreaded sisters.

When I got home, I counted the tip. The sisters had given me $150.

Late that night, reading an article on the Web, I ran across words that seemed to sum up the attitude that the sisters and I had almost instinctively taken to the conflict:

"We are people who really spend too much time thinking about all the awful stuff in the world. . . . We just want to do the right thing, and it matters if we do it the right way."

The right thing, I said to myself.

On the books or off?

The dead-man soap opera didn't end when the job did. Raymond returned to the hall later that week, but balked at repaying the cash. Stella told him he couldn't work there anymore. He stalked out without stopping to say a word to me.

In the ensuing days, my peers asked about the affair. Without saying that I'd leveled with the sisters, I explained the circumstances as best I could. The common opinion was that Raymond and I were fools. As soon as he'd laid the cash on us, we should have told the uncle that we couldn't accept it that day—and offered to return off the books, they said. Nobody felt that we should have continued the job at $7.25 an hour because nobody felt any sympathy for either the sisters or Labor-4-U. Day laborers get their training, not in liberal arts classes where ethics are discussed, but in the School of Hard Knocks.

Only one man took exception to the consensus, an older black guy whom I didn't know, but who claimed he'd been working at the hall, on and off, for more than three years. He said that Raymond was wise. "These people here, they're not that swift. They'd have never caught up with you. Their paperwork ain't that strong," he advised.

I was standing on the front porch a couple of weeks later when Raymond pulled into the parking lot. He walked past a half-dozen guys, straight up to me. I was terrified. But in an entirely gentle way he told me that he had consulted his attorney. Perhaps because they've been arrested a time or two, day laborers commonly have standing relationships with lawyers. His attorney, he told me, was wrangling with Stella and her superiors and had assured Raymond that he'd prevail.

As he talked to me, he kept cutting his eyes into the hall, which he didn't enter. He'd been banned from its grounds.

Perhaps six weeks later, Raymond was back in our ranks. He didn't brag about it, but he claimed that he'd never repaid the cash. Neither Stella nor Dolly ever mentioned the affair to me again. If the sisters were billed or if the uncle sued, I never knew.

13

Handsome and Glib

It was Friday. Dolly gave me and Tony Silvio, the Italian American kid, a ticket for a job that she said was "doing wet seal."

"Mr. Reavis, you are dependable, and Tony, you are as strong as an ox," she said. I was surprised by the compliment.

I had no idea what "wet seal" might be, and neither did Tony. Dolly had given us a Google Maps printout and told us that we could go to the job by bus. Bus fare was a dollar, so we were pleased.

I asked Little Carrie what bus to take. She looked at the instructions and said that we should go to the nearest thoroughfare, ride downtown, and get a transfer to another bus.

Jimmy, the former aspirant to a weekly ticket at the culvert plant, heard me mention "wet seal," and started talking in his staccato way. As always, his speech was difficult to understand, but I got the gist of it.

The previous Wednesday he'd had a ticket to our job where, as nearly as I could make out, he'd been required to work beneath "a trailer." I figured that he meant the kind of trailer that one attaches to a truck. His task involved moving cement bags, or so I understood. Since cement bags weigh eighty pounds, it didn't sound like fun. Jimmy claimed that he had been afraid the trailer would fall on him, and that he'd therefore walked off the job.

I turned to Silvio, who shrugged as if to say, What the heck? What does this guy know?

It was about seven. The job started at eight. We had to wait maybe twenty minutes for the first bus, and perhaps just to kill time, Silvio began telling me his story. He said that he was at Labor-4-U while waiting for his "body to clear," so that he could pass a drug test. He had marijuana in his bloodstream, he said, and he figured that it would take six weeks for its traces to vanish. He didn't tell me why he would be facing a drug test.

The bus took us to a verdant, nearly tropical depot near a square that I had never seen. It was a big place, with lanes both outdoors and under a wall-less roof. Buses came in a half-dozen at a time.

We had to wait for another twenty minutes. Silvio kept talking. He said that he was new to town. In the city where he'd formerly lived he had been a limousine driver, the kind who goes to airports and holds a sign bearing the name of the client that he's to drive. Sometimes, he said, he chauffeured the client for two or three days.

"They told us not to talk to the clients, and I didn't, until they talked to me," he said. "I can understand that, you know. They may have got off a plane from China and been flying for hours, and you know, in that situation, who wants to talk? But if they talked to me, I chatted them up, you know, telling them about the best restaurants and bars and things like that. I was always working them, you know, to get a tip. It's like I told you, man, I hustle!"

I believed his story. He was handsome and glib. It was easy to picture him in a black suit, white shirt, black tie.

He said that he had come to town as part of a scheme. He'd been arrested about a year before when he and a friend were stopped by a patrolman, riding in the friend's car. They'd bailed out and run, but had been caught. In the car the police found six Baggies of heroin.

"They weren't mine, man, but I wasn't going to rat on my friend," Silvio declared. "So I told them that those were mine, for my own personal use."

It was his friend who was dealing heroin, he insisted.

The arrest had led to a lawyer and a series of court dates.

"I showed up in court, clean and dressed in a suit, you know, and I told them I wanted to move here because I had a girlfriend here who I'd gotten pregnant. I told them that I wanted to take care of her and the baby, you know, to get my life back in line."

The truth, he confided, was that he had fathered a boy with a girlfriend in the city where he was arrested. The child was now seven. Silvio said that he was twenty-six. He was still seeing the boy and the mother, who hadn't linked up with anybody else at the time of his arrest.

According to the tale he told, the judge bought his story and sentenced him to six months of probation. If he passed a drug test at the end of that period, he'd be clear of the criminal courts.

He had been in town for the full six months, he said, living in an efficiency apartment that cost $470 a month. He had been at Labor-4-U for three weeks, he said—not two as I had thought.

"Oh, I get it!" I told him. "The guys who owned that heroin agreed to pay your rent and expenses. You didn't have to work," I ventured.

He admitted that that's the way things had been, but rent for his seventh month was facing him. Even with today's pay, he would be forty dollars short on rent money, come Monday.

When we got on the second bus, I told the driver that we needed to get off at or near South East Street. He said that he would notify us, but after we crossed a busy avenue that I knew was beyond the mark, I got worried. Several blocks later I asked him about South East Street. He said that he'd misunderstood me and overshot our destination.

So we waited for a third bus. It took us back toward downtown, and we got off on East, then turned left, according to the Google instructions, and walked for half a mile. We were in a ghetto of sagging seventy- to eighty-year-old houses interspersed with little housing projects.

As we walked, Silvio discoursed about black people. His take was the usual one from whites: Anybody can become anything in the United States, but black families don't raise their children right. The Irish and the Italians built this country, and if they made it, anybody can, et cetera.

He assailed Real Deal, by way of example.

"I worked with him one day, and he was just sitting on the job, him and one of the women. I had to do most of it myself," he complained.

Following the Google instructions, we turned left, or east, and walked about four hundred feet, until we came to a school. Our job was at a school; we knew that. We saw a tradesman's truck there, and going around a corner, saw another pickup. But nobody was in sight.

Silvio handed me his cell phone. I dialed the client's number, which was typed on our ticket, and found out that we were on the wrong side of town. The job was near a shopping center more than five miles from where we stood.

That's when I noticed that the last line of our Google instructions said "Church Street," not 300 Church Street, the address on our ticket. I had used Google enough to know that if it couldn't find a 300 on Church Street, it merely listed the street name. As we would later learn, two Church Streets existed, but only one of them had a 300 number.

By now it was eight, so I called Labor-4-U to see if, since the mistake wasn't ours, someone could drive us in its van. Rush Limbaugh answered the phone. He said that the van was gone. We walked back through the ghetto and got on the bus, going downtown again.

While we were walking the return route and again waiting at the depot, Silvio, apparently having given up on getting a loan from me, was making cell-phone calls to beg for his rent money. After a bit of back-and-forth, his father relented and promised to wire the sum.

By the time we reached the shopping mall, it was nine. I called the client company again, and somebody on the other end of the line gave me directions to the site, some six blocks away. The person with whom I spoke told me to look for a man in a blue hard hat. It was nearly nine thirty when we arrived. We found the man in the blue hard hat.

He told us that the company was based in a town five hundred miles away. It did nothing but erect portable buildings, everywhere. The crew with which we would be working—all of whom were white, I noticed—had that year worked in four states and would soon be in a fifth, the man in the blue hard hat said. He led us to our task, on a patch of land hacked out of the forest. Its red ground had been razed.

The company had joined not truck trailers, but house trailers, side-to-side, to create four buildings, each of nine trailers sixteen feet wide and thirty feet long. The trailers were painted in a greenish brown earth tone. They were going to be used as school buildings.

They sat on stacks of cinder blocks that stood about six feet apart at places, but only about a foot apart at the "mate lines" where the trailers had been "married" one to another. Perhaps a hundred cinder-block columns sat beneath the building to which we were assigned. At one end, the columns stood only two cinder blocks high, about two feet above the ground. Because the ground was sloping, at the opposite end of that building, the trailers stood six blocks high.

The blocks had to be coated or "painted" with a powdery substance, "Surface Bonding Cement," a label on the bags said, that is mixed with water, like concrete. Surface Bonding Cement, the bags said, "provides greater flexural and impact strength." The man in the blue hard hat, William, told me that it eliminated the need for mortar between the cinder blocks. When we applied it, it created a fibrous stucco-like finish. I didn't believe, and still don't believe, that it can replace mortar.

William gave us orange five-gallon buckets and sent us beneath the building to spread the SBC onto the posts.

This wasn't a bad job, Silvio said: The day was hotter than ninety degrees, but it was cool beneath the trailers, and the only things we had to carry under the sun were the buckets of mixed SBC. Our work had to be done on hands and knees, but I figured that, with my bad knee, that was better than standing all day.

The company had failed to tell Labor-4-U, or the hall had failed to tell us, that we needed hard hats to keep from bumping our heads against the steel I-beams that ran along the bottoms of the trailers. Somebody brought Silvio a hard hat.

Because of something that had happened earlier, I always carried one in my backpack, and it was mine. One morning I had checked out a hard hat for a job and, half asleep, had left it lying on the counter. When I'd come in at the end of the day, Jason, the afternoon dispatcher, accused me of having lost it, and threatened to dock my pay by fifteen dollars, about twice the cost at a hardware store. I'd prevailed upon him to telephone Stella, who vouched for my honesty, and Jason had let me go with a warning. I'd bought my own hard hat as soon as I left the hall.

When I went to fill my first bucket, a middle-aged man in khaki pants, khaki shirt, and an engineer's hard hat accosted me. He had a mustache and a sunburned face. He looked like a Brit on safari, I thought.

"Have you ever worked concrete before?" he asked gruffly.

I muttered that I hadn't, afraid that I would be fired from the easy work ahead.

"Well, concrete contains lime and that lime will eat away at your skin. By the end of the day your hands and your arms are going to be red and hurting if you don't wear rubber gloves," he said.

Then he said that he'd get somebody to bring us gloves, and about five minutes later, one of the company's crew brought packets of yellow dishwashing gloves to the edge of the trailer. The man who had accosted me, he said, was the big boss.

A few minutes later, somebody brought a set of badly used knee pads. Silvio said that he didn't need them, so I put them on.

The work was child's play, even if it was dirty. It had rained a day or two before, and the ground beneath the trailers sloped, not only downward, or north, but also west; pools of mud had formed on the western side, and some of the mud had covered the "plates," or cement slabs, beneath the cinder-block columns. Somebody brought hammers. We used their claw ends to dig away the mud, so that from their plates to the wooden shims at their tops, the columns would be covered with SBC.

William, the foreman with the blue hard hat, worked beneath the building with us, "painting" columns himself, and checking to see if we filled the cracks between blocks or missed any spots—which was easy to do, since we were applying gray SBC to columns whose color was only a little bit lighter.

At noon we crawled out to join the other workers—what they had been doing, I never did learn—and the boss man for lunch. Silvio and I rode in the backseat of an extended-cab box truck. We went to a fast-food chicken joint more than a mile away. Silvio, William, and I were caked with dried mud. I was impressed that in the United States, we were allowed inside. In a lot of countries, a guard at the door would have denied us entry.

What a democratic country, I said to myself.

We got in line to order and then took seats, Silvio and I at a table to ourselves. I had loaned Silvio five dollars for lunch, but when the boss man saw that I had ordered only iced tea, he asked if I needed money for lunch.

What a nice guy, I thought. He cares not only about our safety but about whether we have money to eat.

On the drive back, the other guys—there were three in our truck, the oldest of whom was forty-six—began to talk about their jobs. They earned about fifteen dollars an hour, they said, plus a per diem of twenty-five dollars a day. Their motel expenses were paid. All of them were from another state, but they said that they tried to go home for a weekend about once a month. When on a job, they usually worked seven days a week.

I got to thinking about "family values." It all seemed odd to me. William had two stickers on his hard hat. One said "Work Hard, Pray Hard." The other said "Got Jesus?" One of the guys, like William, in his early thirties, had praying hands tattooed on his inner forearm. Did they believe all of the talk from the Christian Right about family values, and if they did, why did they take a job that took them so far from home? They were obviously people who believed that "this is a Christian country"—but would the economy of a Christian country split families for the sake of income?

Of course, these guys cussed like most laborers, and at quitting time, I heard one of them propose to another that they combine their cash resources to buy a bottle of whiskey. From their hard-hat stickers and tattoos, I took them to be members of a teetotaling Baptist, Church of Christ, or Pentecostal sect, but again, I couldn't be sure because of their behavior.

As we were driving back to the work site from lunch, I asked William if his crew was covered by medical insurance.

"You got to understand, this is a new company," he said. "We're less than five years old. That insurance is in the works, they tell us, but it's not time yet."

Nobody groaned or quipped when he said that. From the looks of it, these guys felt that their jobs were a blessing.

Little by little that day, we learned from William what Jimmy's complaint had been. He had been working on the shallow end of the trailers, lying on his back because he didn't have room to kneel, frightened and crying, William said. Another Labor-4-U guy, also an African American, had been working beside him without complaint. Jimmy had telephoned the hall, complaining that the job was dangerous. Dolly had driven out to take a look and decided that it was safe, but she had given Jimmy a ride back to the hall. Thursday she had dispatched two other black guys. William didn't remember any names, but he had not been pleased with their work.

I wondered how long it might take to finish the job. It was less than half done when we arrived. My guess was that nearly a week's work lay ahead.

Once we were again beneath the trailers, I mentioned my speculations to Silvio, who thought for a minute—and began talking up William.

"If you guys want me to, I can come back tomorrow and work fourteen hours, come back Sunday too," he said. "If you'll pay me eight dollars an hour, we can do this off the books, you know."

"Now, that's the kind of talk that I think our boss would like to hear," William told him.

"But eight dollars, that's not enough," I interjected.

"Code for this is eight fifty," William shot back.

"If it's eight fifty, I don't mind taking eight," Silvio told him.

"Eight fifty? I think the going rate for any construction work around here is about twelve or thirteen dollars," I argued.

"Naw, you get plenty of guys for five or six dollars," William said.

I was beginning to dislike this guy. He had already told us that two women had covered the columns in one building in a single day's time, even though we could see that we couldn't work that fast. On one of his trips to fill up his bucket, Silvio had asked the boss man about those two women.

"Yeah, they were Mexican girls, real little, you know," the boss man had said.

But William had told me that the girls were white, or Anglo.

William slipped away for a while and Silvio took the opportunity to lay out his scheme, saying, "Now, you won't tell anybody, will you?" He told me that on every job, he tried to talk his employer into giving him a repeat, off the books.

"I hustle, like I told you," he said.

When William crawled back under the trailers with us, he had a new proposition: that Silvio subcontract the work for the remaining three buildings, at five hundred dollars per building. The company's crew had to leave town for another job on Wednesday, but if Silvio wasn't finished, he could finish after they were gone, William said. The boss man, he promised, would advance him money for the buildings he could finish first, paying the balance when the job was complete.

A few minutes later, William crawled back into the sun and Silvio and I discussed the prospects.

"I don't think I can do it," Silvio said. "I don't have a truck."

But the idea enticed him. He said that he could pay his workers a hundred dollars a day and keep the rest for himself. He figured that two men could do one building in a day.

I told him that I didn't believe the work could go that fast, but he countered with the story of the two girls, which he believed.

I explained that in any case, what he needed were reliable workers and I could think of only two, Henry Hilton and his buddy Wilkins. I meekly said that I was willing to join them, but I knew that I wouldn't, because I didn't believe that the deal would work, even if the workers showed and the boss honestly paid. Besides that, I didn't like working on weekends.

Silvio said that one way or another, he wanted to stay on the job.

"We're getting awful dirty, you know," he allowed, "but I kind of like that. When I go walking down the street, you know, looking like this, I feel like I've done a day's work."

Toward the end of the afternoon, William returned and told Silvio to go talk to the boss. When Silvio came back, he said that he was going to work over the weekend, but on a Labor-4-U ticket. When William signed our ticket, he asked for a repeat for only one worker, for Saturday only.

Only two guys were in the hall when William, on his way to the motel where the crew was staying, dropped us off at about six.

Saturday morning, muscles I didn't know I had were sore. Crawling and working on my back beneath those trailers had done that, but since I took the day off, it didn't really bother me.

Silvio didn't come into the hall Monday. A week later, he showed, saying that he had worked only Saturday at the wet-seal job. But his boots bore red mud.

He said that he hadn't paid his rent and that his electricity had been turned off. But he was planning to return home. A sister who worked for an airline, he said, had arranged for a ticket. He'd be leaving the next day.

Timmy came in that morning for a repeat ticket on a job delivering Sleep Number mattresses to buyers' homes. He'd worked on the job the Friday before, but after standing around for a while—and consulting with Real Deal—he gave his ticket to Silvio, maybe to repay the favor of the dead-man ticket.

I was standing on the porch with them as Timmy was explaining what the assignment entailed. The mattresses came in inflatable segments, he said, which he and the truck driver assembled, then covered with a foam overlay. The set-up work was a breeze, he said; the only hard part of the job was removing old beds from the customers' houses, and that was a chore only if stairs were involved. Four deliveries had been scheduled for Monday, he said, only one of which was an upstairs job.

"What about the driver?" Silvio asked.

"He's a fat guy," Timmy said.

"That's okay. I know plenty of fat-guy jokes," Silvio quipped. Then he turned thoughtful. "I wonder if I can get a tip at each one of those houses?" he asked.

But Timmy wasn't on hand to answer. He and Real Deal had gone to buy cigarettes—or, more likely, a beer—at a convenience store down the street.

14

DEMOLITION

That day we were leveling a small, one-story, rectangular building, thirty feet by twelve feet, inside an abandoned warehouse that had formerly been a repair depot for a home appliance store. The little building, air-conditioned by window units, had apparently been used by supervisors as a shipping and receiving office, and for keeping an eye on warehouse grunts, who labored sans air conditioning. At the front of the building, white-collar employees were still coming to work in cooled cubicles separated from the warehouse expanse by a floor-to-ceiling wall.

Labor-4-U's contract called for three workers. Tyke, the short, middle-aged braggart I knew from the job at the women's-wear store, had been working the ticket for weeks, and he expected it to continue for weeks more. Henry Hilton, the soft-spoken ex-convict who had been on the pavement-popping crew, had put in a couple of days. I was new to the task, which I found taxing, both in body and mind.

At mid-afternoon Henry and I were removing a four-by-three picture window in one of the building's two rooms. We'd already stripped the little office of its roofing, and its other room of windows, gypsum board, or Sheetrock, and plywood, leaving merely a denuded wooden frame. We were starting the same procedure in the remaining room.

Henry had removed the molding that held the picture window in

place from the warehouse side. I stood on that side, ready to grab the
pane on two of its edges when, from inside the room, he tipped it my
way. But he had apparently failed to see and remove one of the tiny
nails that had secured the molding. When he pushed on the glass, it
pivoted, split top to bottom and came falling, slivers of it on both sides
of its frame.

I felt a bump on my hard hat and a blow inside my right wrist as
glass came crashing to the floor in two or three pieces, scattering shards
for five or six feet in every direction. We paused a minute in aston-
ishment, and then, with gloved hands, I started gathering the bigger
pieces and carrying them to a Dumpster outside. Then I got a push
broom and a trash cart and began sweeping the tiny shards.

Henry walked up with a sheet of pasteboard to use as a dustpan.
I noticed, not a lot, but a trickle of blood on one of his forearms, and
I mentioned it. He grinned and pointed at my right arm, where the
blow had landed. Blood was dripping into my glove. I didn't feel any
pain, but I saw a two-inch incision in my shirtsleeve. Beneath it was a
shallow inch-long cut in my forearm. Henry shrugged off his wound,
smaller than mine, but I went to the front of the building to find a first-
aid kit, feeling lucky that no artery had been hit.

Our boss man was a subcontractor, and our contract was with him,
not with the appliances chain. He saw me walking toward the white-
collar offices. A gaunt white man in his late fifties, he had hovered
behind us all day, observing and scolding—when he wasn't outside
smoking, that is. I had watched him take long, deep drags on his cigarettes and hold the smoke in his lungs as long as he could, as I had once
done—and still wished I could do. I wondered if his lungs were in better shape than mine, but of course, since he hadn't been banging and
pulling with the three of us, I hadn't been able to observe his breathing
under physical strain.

A first-aid kit was just inside the door that led to the cubicles. After
wiping my cut with antiseptic, I slapped a bandage across it and went
back to work. The boss was sitting in a chair, watching me. He said
nothing, but I suspect that's when he made up his mind.

He had been keeping a skeptical eye on me all day. It started early in the morning. Tyke was on the warehouse floor, carrying detritus to the outdoor Dumpster. Henry and I had gone up a wooden stairway on the north side of the building to reach its flat roof, built of three-quarter-inch plywood. Apparently, the roof had been used to store boxes and old machinery; several strips of cardboard and an abandoned window unit were still on top. We dragged the window unit downstairs and carried it to the Dumpster, then returned to strip the plywood.

Our tools were a nail puller, a three-foot and a two-foot crowbar, a short-handled and a long-handled sledgehammer, and an ordinary claw hammer. One by one, we pulled nails from the edges of the four-by-eight-foot plywood sheets until we could slip the crowbars beneath them. Then we pried the sheets upward, lifting nails as we went. As each nail popped free, it set loose a puff of dust. When we had removed a sheet, we dropped it to the floor, where Tyke carried it away.

It took us about an hour to remove the plywood sheets, leaving the roof's two-by-four and two-by-six skeleton exposed. Standing on the skeleton's bars, Henry began banging on the roof's framing with the short-handled sledgehammer, breaking beams away. I went downstairs to help Tyke.

He was wearing a Yankees baseball cap and a pair of safety eyeglasses. He warned me to don mine, which were in my backpack, against the wall that separated the offices from the warehouse. On my way there, something occurred to me. Henry was pounding on the trusses, which broke in chunks. Tyke and I were working beneath him. I decided to get not only my safety glasses, but my hard hat as well. Neither Dolly nor our boss man had mentioned a need for safety equipment, but it seemed apparent that with someone working overhead, even steel-toe boots, which I'd never bought, might have been a good idea.

I went back to the task with Tyke, and at morning break, the three of us and the boss man took chairs onto the loading dock outside. Leaning back in his chair and puffing on a cigarette, the boss man took a long look at me.

"There's just one thing I want to say," his gravelly voice grumbled. "You can wear that hard hat, or you can't."

I wondered why he'd said that, and I explained why I was wearing it. He didn't respond.

After the break, Henry finished stripping the roof and joined Tyke and me on the floor. While Tyke hauled away the debris, Henry and I started denuding the building's walls. On the outside, they were of quarter-inch plywood, nailed to studs. We pulled nails from the molding that seemingly held the plywood in place, but underneath it, we found more nails, smaller than those upstairs, more difficult to locate and not much easier to remove.

The walls inside the room were of Sheetrock, which our sledge-hammers could puncture with a single swing. We began knocking holes in the Sheetrock, and from the building's inside, banging on the quarter-inch plywood. That loosened its nails and made the plywood easier to remove.

I noticed that with each hammer bang and each tug on the plywood or Sheetrock, small clouds of dust arose. Not wanting to aggravate the low-level bronchitis that, doctors say, is chronic with COPD, I went to my backpack and pulled out an air-filter mask. Within minutes, because I was sweating, the mask was wet and I was gasping for air.

That's when I remembered a gift from my wife, Miriam. The air masks that Labor-4-U and a few clients provided were simple paperish devices that cost about two dollars each. Miriam had bought me a five-dollar mask with a little plastic valve in its center. I went to my backpack, switched masks, and returned to my chores. Even when, half an hour later, the new mask was damp with sweat, I could breathe, thanks to the valve. The boss man noticed me wearing the mask, but he didn't say a word.

Henry and I were tearing out the walls faster than Tyke could carry their components away. We stopped to help him catch up. The Dumpster outdoors was nearly full on its dock side. We had to hurl sheets of plywood and molding, javelin-style, to get them to the far side, which was emptier. After we'd made a couple of trips, the boss man came onto the dock to supervise.

"Throw all of that stuff toward the back!" he bellowed when I arrived with a new load—as if I didn't know the obvious procedures for throwing away junk.

One of the office workers appeared and called Tyke aside to show him a refrigerator that was stocked with frozen dinners. A microwave oven also sat against the office-warehouse wall. Tyke scurried to tell Henry and me, and the three of us broke for lunch. The boss man said that when we finished eating, rather than return to stripping the little building's rooms, we should remove its stairway.

When we started that undertaking, my instinct was to pry away the molding first, to dismantle the stairway from outside in, reversing the order of its construction. The boss man was watching as I stripped the molding away. He picked up a long crowbar, stabbed it through the thin plywood, and used it to pry loose the sheeting, which brought the molding with it. His more physical procedure was more efficient, I could see. I finished the job his way.

After we'd stripped the stairway to its frame, it dawned on us that the stairs were carpet-clad. With crowbars we lifted the carpeting, creating clouds of dust that dimmed the warehouse from end to end. But the boss wasn't troubled by that because he was on the dock, smoking a cigarette.

A few minutes later Henry felled one of the walls of framing in the first room. It was too big to carry to the Dumpster. With a crowbar, I began trying to separate its members. The boss man sauntered in, picked up a sledgehammer, and used it to knock apart two of its arms. Then he handed the sledgehammer to me, sneered, and walked off. He was right, of course. The hammer made the job easier.

I suspected that he already had me in his book as a safety freak and a greenhorn. And that was before the window fell.

At three thirty, quitting time, we telephoned the hall because we didn't have a ride. "Rush Limbaugh" came for us in the van. Tyke loaded into it three or four boxes of copper wiring, which the boss had allowed him to save from the demolition. Copper was selling for about three dollars a pound, Tyke said, and he bragged that after scavenging on the job the week before, he'd sold his haul for just pennies less than a hundred dollars.

On the drive to the hall, Limbaugh said in a voice that was almost meek, "Pops, the man back there called this afternoon and told me that he didn't want you back tomorrow."

I didn't comment.

"Man, what did you say to him?" Limbaugh pressed.

"Not much," I muttered.

"I don't know why he'd do that. You be working," Tyke said, to my surprise.

"Yeah, you worked," Henry added.

"It may be because a couple of times, he saw that I didn't know what I was doing," I said, without mentioning the scorn that the boss man had shown for my safety gear—and without mentioning the cut on my arm.

In any case, I didn't care. The job was dusty and dangerous and I didn't like the boss.

Henry had the ticket. Back at the hall, he glanced at it before dropping it into the "pay" basket that sat on the counter. He called me to his side.

"Man, look at what that guy did to you!" he exclaimed.

Taking the ticket in hand, I saw that the boss man had given Henry and Tyke credit for ten hours, and me, only nine.

The following morning, Dolly called Tyke and Henry for their repeat, and pointing out a younger white worker, asked Tyke if the guy could handle the job. Tyke walked up and down the hall a couple of times, and in a voice that everyone heard, pronounced the worker unfit.

"Why are you saying that?" the guy protested.

"Because yesterday Pops got called on that ticket, and he couldn't cut the mustard, so I know you can't," he hollered.

At the expense of my reputation and that of the other worker, Tyke was playing boss man again.

15

THE FESTIVAL

Our job was at an expansive, municipally owned wooded park in the suburbs, where a traveling festival, Booze, Burgers, and Blues, was being staged. Admission was by ticket only, and tickets were pricey: Only well-scrubbed white folks in their thirties were in attendance, probably two thousand of them. As we came into the park about an hour before sundown, they were beginning to leave, streaming into its parking lot in clumps of two, four, and six. In my memory, male and female, they were all dressed alike: white tennis shirts, khaki pants, and sunglasses, with fancy baseball caps on their heads. Some of them carried slices of pizza between the folds of paper towels because the festival had run out of meat and its promoters had ordered more than fifty cheese pizzas, free to the takers, by way of apology.

Many of the exiting guests were carrying souvenir glasses emblazoned with the festival's logo; one glass came with each ticket. Most were filled with bourbon, wine, or beer. A couple of security guards and a policeman stood at the entry-exit gate, but they halted no one.

"Man, if these folks were black, the cops would be on top of them!" somebody on our crew noted. Others voiced agreement with him, even amazement. Getting into a car with an open container of booze, even walking into a public parking lot with booze in hand, were violations of public safety laws, as any acquaintance of Real Deal already knew.

When we explained our purpose to the guards, they pointed us to a fat white man who sat behind an aluminum table just beyond the gate. He motioned us in, and as we neared his table, a young blonde at an adjoining table tossed a T-shirt at each one of us. The shirts were pastel blue. On their backs they carried the words "Event Staff." We donned them and, following the fat man's directions, walked along a paved path that led inside the park. Blues music, at least as contemporary rockers interpret it, was playing in the air.

Saturdays are different at labor halls. The mix of personnel changes in favor of workers who have forty-hour jobs and perform weekend labor only to supplement their incomes. Because the hall closes before sundown on Saturdays, dispatchers issue a ticket to each worker. Regulars collect on Mondays, but weekend workers usually wait for the Saturday that follows.

That morning I'd been assigned to the festival job with four others, only one of whom I knew. The job wasn't set to start until 5:00 p.m.; we agreed to meet at the hall at four.

The new faces were those of a tightly wound young black man who went by the nickname Wolfie, and our drivers for the job, a fleshy husband-and-wife team, also African Americans, who called themselves Daddy and Honey. Gary, a black guy in his fifties, I already knew. He had been at Labor-4-U for about three years and we had worked together on a half-dozen jobs, including the one where I'd contracted the flu. I'd learned to take everything he said about his past with a grain of salt. He claimed that he made most of his living buying and selling used cars, and that for a time he had supervised forty-eight people at a warehouse. But he came to the hall every day.

The trail we were following ended at a vast open space, a valley bordered by a lake and surrounded by rises. A bandstand twenty-five yards long had been built with its back to the lake; musicians stood atop it, playing and singing into microphones. Festivalgoers stood beneath it, gazing upward in awe, booze-filled glasses in their hands. Only a dozen people were dancing, but hundreds lay or sat on the lawns, wagging their heads and grooving.

On the rise opposite the lake were perhaps a dozen rows of permanent bleachers, cast in concrete. A steel canopy shielded the last half-dozen rows, and beneath it, vendors displayed their wares on aluminum tables: music CDs, bottles of wine, soft drinks, and beer. Gardening and home repair companies had taken tables, too, probably because most of the people in the crowd were first- and second-time home buyers.

Between the bleachers and the lake sat a mammoth open-air tent of thick white vinyl. Beneath it no fewer than thirty barmaids were serving beer and drinks to lines of festivalgoers at counters on the edges of the tent. In smaller white tents that dotted the ridges, vendors dispensed beverages, proffered services, or sold souvenirs. We were in the middle of a big yuppie blowout.

We reported to a muscled, thirtyish black foreman who called himself Monk. Our job, he said, would be to close the festival, packing the gear its promoters had brought and loading it onto a truck. He pointed to the inside of the tent. Plastic tubes snaked across its grassy floor, where dozens of steel bottles of carbon dioxide, used for carbonated drinks, and about a hundred beer kegs stood. Gesturing toward the entrance, he said, "Now, the first thing I want you to do is get those gas bottles uphill."

We started toting.

The bottles, between three and four feet high and about fifteen inches in diameter, were unwieldy and ponderous. Only Daddy could carry two at a time. After a couple of trips, he somewhere found a hand truck on which he was able to move five at once! Trudging up the hill, we left the bottles near a Dumpster on a concrete pad surrounded by a brick wall. We finished transferring them about six, the festival's closing time.

The barmaids, mostly white women in their late twenties who, one of them told us, had been hired through a classified ad, vanished in an instant. It took longer for the festivalgoers to stagger out.

The ground beneath the tent was sodden and spongy. Most of the hundred kegs of beer sat in short red plastic barrels filled with ice. We dumped the barrels onto the lawn, then placed them, one into another, in a dozen stacks, tossing plastic pitchers into the top barrel on each stack.

The counters on the tent's four sides had been covered with black vinyl cloths. At Monk's instruction, we folded and placed these in a stack on the ground.

Dozens of boxes of wine, and of canned and bottled beer, were also beneath the tent; we moved them to a central spot. Up on the hills, we collapsed folding tables and the little tents; it was easy, since the tents were one-piece contraptions that, accordion-like, folded into bundles at a touch.

Monk and another member of the festival's traveling crew, Davis, drove up to the big tent in what they called Gators. But the vehicles looked to me like mere golf carts with boxlike beds, protected by railings behind their bench seats. Monk and Davis disappeared into the descending darkness and returned again, a few minutes later, with two more carts. We loaded boxes and buckets and barrels into their beds, and the two of them, plus a couple of us, began making runs in the carts toward the bandstand, where Monk had parked a truck with a long, rectangular box. The drivers unloaded their cargo beside the truck and let it sit.

The kegs and boxes of beer that remained beneath the tent were naturally a temptation. One guy filled a pitcher with bock beer and drove his cart with one hand, using the other to swill. In less than an hour, Gary popped the tops on a half-dozen cans of Heineken, all the while prompting Davis, the festival crewman, to accompany him on a tour of nightclubs when the job was finished. As he sipped and spun, his stories grew taller. He said that he'd once been a valet parking attendant, earning five thousand dollars in tips during a single December. Before long, he was telling us that Heineken is specially brewed so as to forestall drunkenness and hangovers. Daddy and I, the only teetotalers in the lot, openly expressed our disbelief.

On-the-job boozing was taking its toll, I saw, when one of the drivers came skidding into the tent on his cart. Nobody fell off while driving, but a couple of drivers, now carrying passengers who leaned out of the door-less carts waving challenges to one another, nearly collided in an impromptu race to the truck.

Monk was tippling, too, so nobody got scolded. But others noticed.

Six Mexican workers, five men and one woman, had appeared in the bleachers, sweeping trash and carting it away. After a while, one by one the men filed into our tent, each asking for a beer. Several came back more than once, and we rewarded them each time. One of the Mexicans told me that his crew, employed by a cleaning service, had worked the same bleachers the night before—until 3:00 a.m.

About eight, we brought down the big tent, which folded into neat sections that we bound with Velcro straps. Thirty minutes later, all of us were standing around the truck, toting barrels and boxes and folded tents to its power lift. Monk and Davis stood inside, putting each piece of gear in its place. When everything was loaded, Monk got into the cab and told us to meet him at the entrance gate.

Boxes of T-shirts and souvenir liquor glasses were stacked atop its half-dozen folding aluminum tables. We carried the merchandise and the tables to the truck. Just outside the gate stood a cash-dispensing machine, property of the touring company. We unplugged it, and with the aid of a dolly and a good deal of brute strength, squeezed it into the truck too. The last item we loaded, hidden in an indoor office near the entryway, was the company's safe. It took two of us to wrestle it onto a hand truck, and only Daddy could move it away.

On the drive over, he and Honey had chatted with the rest of us. It was clear from what they said that they had never worked at the hall before, and that, on weekdays, Daddy had a construction job. My impression was that the couple had come to Labor-4-U in hopes of earning funds to cover an emergency need. Somebody had told them that each rider in their car—three of us—would owe five dollars at the end of the job, our fare. But it was nearly midnight when we returned. The hall was closed and wouldn't reopen until Monday. Nobody had money to pay Daddy and his wife except me, and since Saturday workers are not regulars, it's a good guess that they never collected the rest of their fares.

16

THE END

I am not a religious man, but perhaps I should have known that the end was coming. The day had started out badly when, in the woods, I encountered a guy who called himself Satan.

I had pushed my wheelbarrow, carrying two-by-two squares of sod, down the yard's long incline, beneath a cluster of trees and through a chain-link gate into the untamed woods where I was supposed to dump the sod. A worker I knew only by an uncomplimentary nickname stood just beyond the gate. His wheelbarrow had tipped and spilled perhaps fifteen squares of sod onto the ground.

I knew why that had happened to him because I'd already made two or three trips from the yard. The ground in the woody area was uneven, eroded by flows of rainwater. Natural debris—twigs, branches, and stones—diverted the barrow's wheel too. We had to wrestle a wheelbarrow to get it to the area, about fifteen yards inside the woods, where we were supposed to dump.

Looking over my shoulder to make sure that neither the boss man nor our client was watching, I pushed my wheelbarrow alongside that of my coworker, who was picking up the spilled squares. I was going to tell him that I'd found that I couldn't navigate the woods with a load of more than ten squares, and to show him that I carried only five. Giving him advice was in my interest, since I didn't want to look—to the boss or the client—like a slacker.

"Say, brother, what's your name?" I asked.

"Satan!" he spat.

"I know that you're not happy this morning, but really, what is your name?" I pressed.

"Like I told you, Satan."

He glared at me with burning yellow-brown eyes, as if he were ready to fight. I stepped back.

I knew the guy, though only in passing. He was small, butternut-colored, and in his early thirties, no taller or huskier than I am. His mannerisms were delicate, and when he was in a good mood—as had been the case every time I'd heard him speak until that morning—he had a delicate manner of speech. In the hall he always sat with the women workers. The guys referred to him by a nickname they'd bestowed: Eggshell Tinker Bell, or Tinker Bell for short.

That morning the five on our crew, including Timmy, whom I knew from the dead-man job, had come to work in the old Caprice that belonged to the wife of Henry Hilton, my buddy from the pavement-popping and demolition jobs. Satan, as he was now calling himself, had been riding shotgun when a song playing from a CD, something about a guy who was remorseful for mistreating his ex-wife, set him off.

Two minutes earlier, he had been practically dancing in the front seat, and for our entertainment, I suppose, hailing women we passed with greetings like, "Honey, baby, you are hot!"

But when he heard that song, he talked back to it, repeating conversations that he'd had with a wife whom he said he had divorced months earlier.

"That bitch, she wouldn't put out when I wanted her," he growled. "And the worst of it was that she got away with my seven-hundred-dollar flat-screen TV. The bitch didn't even leave me the box! She did leave me the Styrofoam, though," he said, irony competing with hatred.

Then he added that he wanted to throw lye in her face, and for good measure, onto the face of his ex-mother-in-law.

Though we had found his retelling of bedroom woes a bit amusing, nobody knew how to respond when his talk turned violent; a couple of guys had chuckled and a couple had rolled their eyes. It was hard to tell if Tinker Bell was truly enraged, or if he was performing, trying to upstage Real Deal as chief comic in the car.

"Man, I feel like burning this whole place down. Just toss me a match, use my lighter, set these woods on fire!" he said as we stood by the wheelbarrows.

I pushed on, hoping he'd leave his lighter in his pocket.

Fifteen minutes later, I heard him telling the boss man about "that bitch," while threatening to do her mischief. And he kept up the Satan act all morning. By noon, Real Deal was calling him Mephistopheles and Lucifer.

"And you're one of my minions," Satan said.

Real Deal understood the term.

We were working in an exurban development of new mansions with 7,500-square-foot floor plans and $1.5–$2 million price tags. The backyard of our client's two-and-a-half-story mansion was the biggest I'd ever seen. From the rear of the house, it sloped downward for yards and yards, until it came to a grove bounded on its far side by a chain-link fence. The woods started beyond the fence.

Standing in the grove at the rear of the yard as I returned uphill with my wheelbarrow, I tried to estimate the grassy expanse, compared to my own spacious lawn, which, with a push-mower, takes about an hour to cut. I figured that our client's lawn—the backyard only—would take at least nine hours.

While I was eyeballing it, the homeowner, a middle-aged white man in a pastel tennis shirt, came up.

"I'm trying to figure," I told him. "Is your backyard closer to fifty or a hundred yards long?"

"Oh, it's a hundred yards," he said, as if that kind of spread was entirely commonplace.

Real Deal already knew the client and the place. He had worked there about four months earlier, sodding, he said. Some of the grass hadn't "taken," and the landscaper who was our boss was bound by his contract to replace the dead squares. Four pallets of sod, each about six by five, stood in the homeowner's driveway at the elevated end of the backyard.

The whole expanse had an automatic watering system, yet it was dry. The dead spots were yellowed, and the healthy parts of the lawn, not heartily green. We cut into the dusty turf with flat shovels, then pushed down on their handles, prying the dead grass free, then tossing it and the inch or two of dirt that clung to its roots into our wheelbarrows. But after every yellow spot we lifted, we noticed that neighboring patches were on their way to dying too. We had started about eight, and by ten, it was apparent that before we were done, we'd have to dig up a third of the yard.

We were not the only workers on the job. Three guys on the boss man's regular crew were helping: a fifty-year-old from Mexico City, a sixteen-year-old student from an elite high school—for him, this was a summer vacation job—and Dudley, a shaggy white guy, probably in his late thirties, who was already known to some of us because the boss had hired him from a Labor-4-U crew six months earlier. The trio complained that ours was the toughest job they'd had; their usual work was mowing.

The boss man was a thirtyish weight-lifter blond who constantly circled behind us, pointing to patches that needed removal and exhorting us to "get a move on it!"—an utterance whose real content, I thought, was, You guys are the coolies and I'm the prince. His regular crewmen told us that he never granted them breaks, and Real Deal recalled that when he'd helped sod the place, the crews hadn't stopped for lunch.

About mid-morning, when the sun started to blaze, I scanned the rear of the house and its backyard, but hadn't been able to spot a faucet. Henry Hilton walked onto its patio but couldn't find an outlet either.

About that time, one of our crew, Maceo, an African American in his late twenties, hollered, "We need a cooler!" From the way he shouted, I couldn't tell if he was joking or demanding.

"Yeah, but where would I get one?" the boss man replied.

"At Lowe's," Maceo said, citing the name of a building materials chain.

Shortly the boss man disappeared without saying a word. Apparently, the homeowner had heard the brief exchange, because as soon as the boss vanished, he came out of his kitchen, on an elevated first floor, bringing plastic bottles of cold Gatorade.

Within an hour the boss man returned with a cooler. It didn't look new to me.

Using the empty Gatorade bottles as cups, we formed a line at the cooler. But we were dismayed: Its water was lukewarm.

"Why don't you put some ice in the water?" Maceo asked. His voice was both low and polite—as if he were pleading.

"You? Complaining again?" the boss man snapped. "Do you want to go home? I'll send you!"

He pulled a cell phone out of a pocket and dialed the labor hall.

After speaking for a minute or two, he handed his phone to Maceo. Dolly, or perhaps Stella, was on the other end of the line. Everyone stopped working to watch. I drew close to listen.

"I didn't refuse to work!" Maceo was saying. "If you want to put me off the job, that's okay. But I didn't tell him that I wouldn't work!"

Then he gave back the phone, and the boss man began talking to the hall, walking away as he did. As soon as the boss was out of our hearing, Maceo said that he'd been told that if he didn't finish the ticket, nobody would come to get him until four—and he'd be suspended for ten days.

Word traveled to everyone on the crew. I expected Real Deal to tell us to lay down our tools until ice came, but like the others, he only muttered something and shrugged. All of us kept shoveling.

About noon the homeowner and his wife came out of their kitchen with bags from a fast-food outlet, hamburgers with french fries. They placed them, with cups of iced soft drinks, on glass-topped tables that sat on a small patio at the rear of the house. The boss man had no choice; he had to let us stop for lunch.

The man of the mansion sat on the patio with us. When Real Deal moaned about shovel work causing pain in his lower back, the homeowner went into his kitchen and came back with a bottle of Aleve, which we passed from hand to hand. Real Deal swallowed a couple of tablets, and when we went back to work—at the boss's order, a mere twenty minutes later—he traded his shovel for a wheelbarrow. I paired myself with the student and told him that barrow-wrestling had inflamed my bad knee. He agreed to let me shovel while he ferried.

Standing over us that afternoon, the boss man went into a long tirade about being unable to find reliable employees "these days" because "nobody wants to work anymore." I thought it presumptuous of him that at age thirty or thirty-two, he thought he could voice old-timer complaints. He followed with a rant about the aimlessness of "workers today": Why, he said, he'd set up a 401(k) plan for his regular employees, but none of them wanted to contribute.

By this time, practically whispering as we shoveled and loaded, we had learned that Dudley, the Labor-4-U hire, was earning eight dollars an hour, and the Mexican, who'd been with the boss for a year, earned ten fifty. The boss man was out of touch with reality: With wages like theirs, who could afford contributions to a retirement plan?

I thought that the boss was disparaging the nation's workforce merely so as to say, "Keep humping. I'm still the boss." But apparently, that wasn't the point: In his delusion, he seemed to think that the 401(k) plan was an attraction to potential employees; he mentioned that he'd been shorthanded for the past several weeks, as if enticing us to join his crew.

"I'm a landscaper!" Hilton hollered.

"Yeah, but I know you Labor-4-U guys," the boss said, nodding toward Dudley. "None of you wants to work hard."

"I'm a Labor-4-U guy, and I admit, you're right," I interjected. "I don't want to work hard, but this guy here, I've worked plenty of jobs with him, and he does work hard."

The boss man's eyes followed my pointing finger. He looked Henry up and down, but said nothing: My tout didn't take.

The afternoon was short. We quit at three, having clocked eight hours. On our way back to the hall, Henry stopped at a convenience store, perhaps a half-mile from the mansion. Real Deal and Satan went in.

Satan came out first, fuming because the "white bitch" attendant had "slammed the change into my hand." He added that "her guts could be on fire and I wouldn't throw any water on her."

Real Deal emerged with two twenty-four-ounce cans of 211. He was wearing an army fatigue shirt, open at the waist. The attendant, he said, had told him to button the shirt; he'd given her the finger and spoken a few choice words. The reports of the two frightened Henry. He was afraid that the lady—or maybe the racist lady—had called the police. He sped out of the place.

When we got back to the hall and went to the counter, Jason, the afternoon dispatcher, decided that we deserved a little lecture.

"Boys, it is your responsibility to provide food and drinks for yourself," he began. "If your boss doesn't provide you a cooler, you should be prepared for that."

"But on every job where you've got that many guys, they put out a cooler," Maceo protested.

Somebody else asked how we were supposed to provide water for ourselves.

"It's easy," Jason proclaimed. "You get a gallon jug tonight. You put water in it and freeze it. Then tomorrow you take it out there in the sun and it melts."

Didn't he know, I asked myself, that a lot of his workers didn't have kitchens or freezers—and that some didn't have homes?

Somebody else said that on hot days, a gallon of water wouldn't be enough.

"Then you take two gallons," Jason said, not budging an inch.

The idea was nonsense. Five of us had gone to the job that day. Was Henry to have carried ten or twelve gallons of water in his trunk? If seven of us had been hired, he was to haul fifteen or twenty gallons?

As I walked away from the hall a fiftyish white man whom I'd seen on the porch was following me. He caught up with me a half-block away. He'd been to a nearby labor hall but hadn't scored a ticket, he said. He wanted to know if work was plentiful at Labor-4-U. I told him that things there were pretty fine.

He hadn't taken the employment test, and when I told him about it, he frowned.

"Look, I just got out of prison two days ago. It hasn't been a year," he explained. I encouraged him to take the test and to lie, because my impression had been that nobody checked on the answers we gave.

"All you really need is two forms of ID—a Social Security card and a government ID of some kind," I told him.

"I've got a Social Security card and a government ID," he said with a chuckle. "But it's my prison ID."

I suggested that he go to an office of the state's driver's license authority and get, not a license, but a simple identification card.

"But that costs fifteen dollars," he told me, "and to get that, I'd have to work."

I didn't reach into my pocket to solve his problem, and we parted ways. Early the following morning, as I was going to work, I saw him standing outside the plasma center, waiting to sell his blood.

All of us except Maceo had been listed on a repeat ticket for the landscaping job, and when we gathered, Satan was begging Real Deal not to repeat a scene from the day before. After the hall paid us, he said, Real Deal had bought a third can of 211, popped its top, and boarded a city bus with him.

"You can't drink on the bus," its woman driver had barked at him.

"Yes, I can, because I work!" he retorted.

The bus driver picked up her microphone and called her dispatching office to ask for the police. Real Deal calmly took a seat with Satan, who was rattled.

"But I knew I could drink because I was going to get off before the cops had time to catch our bus," he told us that morning.

By the time a patrol car halted the bus, Real Deal had exited, Satan said, leaving him alone to explain.

On the drive to the mansion, we stopped at the convenience store. I paid for two bags of ice and put them in Henry's trunk. Real Deal bought another can of 211, boasting that he could drain it in 10.3 seconds. He had done as much by the time we reached the mansion.

Two of the four pallets of sod remained, but the day would be a short one, the boss man said. We were to finish the job by noon, come what may. Henry had told him about a machine for stripping sod from the ground, and when we arrived, the boss was already out back, operating the machine. A morning's rental had cost him eighty dollars, he said.

He had already made plenty of cuts, so the noon deadline didn't seem impossible. The boss's cooler was sitting on the lawn, but it was nearly dry. I put my ice inside and we went to work.

The boss told us to lay new sod into the strips that he had cleared. Some men were to ferry the sod from the driveway to the yard, while the others would lay it in, he said. I turned to the yard, planning to do lay-in work, but he pointed me toward a wheelbarrow. My knee was inflamed, I told him. Without scowling or arguing, he said that I could load sod for the wheelbarrow men.

I took a position by the pallets, and as the others came to me, tossed squares of turf into their barrows. Before long, I began counting them in. Satan had apparently taken my advice: He took loads of only seven squares. Two or three guys traded tasks on a second wheelbarrow, usually carrying loads about twice as big. But Real Deal had me toss turf until he told me to stop, usually only when it had risen a foot above the wheelbarrow's bucket with twenty-five to thirty squares. And then, every time, he went pushing his barrow at a run. After he'd made several trips, I calculated: Three guys were pushing wheelbarrows, but he was delivering at least 75 percent of the sod!

During the first hour, the boss man's cell phone rang every ten or fifteen minutes. He'd stop his machine, take the call, and then holler a report to the rest of us. He was talking to Dudley, who said he was having car trouble. He described his mechanical trouble to the boss, who suggested remedies, but nothing worked. Finally he told the boss that he'd telephoned a towing service.

"His car is probably running fine," the boss man commented. "I think the guy has substance problems." Nobody challenged his verdict, and it apparently didn't occur to him that it was likely that a guy earning eight dollars an hour couldn't afford a reliable car.

Our understanding was that we had to be finished by noon because the householders were hosting a wedding that day. At mid-morning the door on the mansion's garage rolled electronically into its ceiling. The client stepped out with two young women he introduced as his daughters, college-age blondes. One was talking on a cell phone as she leaned against a small white sedan, parked in the driveway. The other stood aside, waiting.

Real Deal and Satan were at the pallets for reloading. They unashamedly leered at the daughters. Deal stepped toward them, asking where they were going and if he could join them. One of them said they were headed to a nail salon.

"Oh, but I am a manicurist!" Satan exclaimed, skipping toward the pair. He held out his arms, letting his hands droop, nail side out. The girls shrugged, got into the car, and left.

The loads for Satan and Deal were practically the last of the job. I started sweeping away dirt and debris. Everybody soon gathered on the driveway to hoist wheelbarrows and shovels into the boss man's pickup. Real Deal was cajoling him to give us credit for eight hours instead of four. He gave us six and I told myself that if a new ticket came for work on his crew, despite the friction over breaks, lunch, and water, I might be willing to return. All of us stepped over and shook his hand.

"I sure love working for you," Henry said, practically begging for a job.

But as before, the boss man didn't take the cue.

When we got to the hall, Jason asked if any of us knew how to drive a street-sweeper truck. Henry Hilton and the white boy Timmy scrambled to the counter.

"The job will run for more than a month, maybe turn into something permanent. But it's at night, eight thirty at night to six thirty in the morning," Jason told them.

Timmy slunk back. Henry said that he'd take the ticket.

The two laborers whom I had come most to admire were Real Deal, for his absurd and uncooperative view of life, and in a more serious way, Henry, the gentle but strong everyman. Sadly, I never saw Henry again after he took the street-sweeping job.

His departure added to an embarrassment and a moment of self-realization that had come on the first morning of the landscaping job, right before Satan told me his name.

I had made my first wheelbarrow trip into the woods, fully loaded with fifteen or twenty squares. Going back up the incline toward the yard got the best of me. The barrow's wheel had slowed when it came upon the matting of pine needles and oak leaves on the grove's floor. I had to exert myself to keep it moving, and I found myself short of breath.

Panting, I halted and leaned forward, resting my weight on the wheelbarrow's handlebars. I had heard somebody on my right, up in the yard, holler, "Pops, are you okay?" To my left I saw another comrade trotting in my direction.

I raised my head and nodded, and everyone saw that I was fine.

"Huh, don't scare us like that," the man on my right said. "We thought you were having a heart attack."

Then my interlocutor—I was too dizzy to clearly see him—asked me if I'd rather take a shovel and leave the barrow work to him.

I didn't accept the offer, but in that instant, old, white, and antisocial as I was, I realized that my coworkers cared about whether I lived or died. I hadn't expected as much and I am not sure that I would have felt the same compassion had our roles been reversed.

The concern of my coworkers impressed me. In a nation of anonymous, atomized individuals, either from curiosity or what might be called class or species feeling—remarkably, somebody still gave a damn! For once I felt that I belonged, that I had somehow earned a niche in a collectivity. I was somehow valued by my coworkers, not for my stamina or skills—both of which were under par—but because, at least at that moment, I was trying to do my best. I had made the grade. My worries, going back decades, that I'd never be accepted as a "regular" in a blue-collar milieu, were apparently over—though, of course, I'd never brought a book to the job!

That realization gave me confidence. I no longer had to show at the hall every morning, I decided. My comrades, I assumed, would always be there and I would be welcome among them, not as long as my health was good—something the incident placed in doubt—but ostensibly, as long as I was willing to make an effort. If I fell short, others would take up the slack for me. I was like the blind man at the chemical plant, or like Lester. Somebody was looking out for me.

But since I wasn't really unemployed, I began to feel obligated to my peers too. I felt that it wasn't quite fair, if they accepted my limitations, to compete with them for bread and beer. I didn't need day-labor wages nearly as badly as they. I began to feel that I shouldn't show up until I was truly short of cash—maybe when I retired.

Within two or three weeks, I quit reporting to Labor-4-U, though even now I drop by from time to time, just to keep up with gossip. Since the lives of ordinary working people tend to be routine, I have little of dramatic interest to report, with the exception of one incident.

About 3:15 one Friday afternoon, at the end of a workday some six weeks after we finished the landscaping job, Real Deal came into the hall with a crew of others to collect his pay. But that afternoon, according to eyewitnesses, his joviality didn't seem cute so much as menacing. His black eyes were glowing, everyone could see.

"He's got something more than beer in him," one of the women observed.

Deal and his minions began creating a ruckus. People couldn't hear the television because of the uproar.

"Rush Limbaugh" was on duty. He told Real Deal and his claque to be quiet. They obeyed, but only for a minute or two.

He warned them again. They went quiet, for a minute again.

Rush told them a third time.

Real Deal stood up and started giving him lip.

"If you don't sit down and shut up, I am going to fire you and call the police," Rush threatened.

Real Deal froze defiantly, a universal and old hatred for Limbaugh in his eyes.

Limbaugh reached for the telephone.

Real Deal stomped outside, then turned on the porch to continue his backtalk.

As if he'd been waiting on the nearest corner, a cop immediately drove up. His report stated he thought he saw Deal stick something into the pocket of his Black Panther coat. When the cop questioned him, Real Deal wasn't respectful, and in the blink of an eye the cop pinned him to the ground, his knee in Deal's back. But the cop couldn't move him away. Reaching for a walkie-talkie at his waist, he called for backup.

Three cars with flashing lights came into the parking lot. Cops dashed out. When they let Real Deal rise, he hollered and fought, kicking off a shoe as, pressing his arms to his sides, they crammed him into the backseat of a patrol car, separated from the driver's compartment by a heavy metal screen. It took five cops to arrest Real Deal at the labor hall. When they searched his coat, the report stated, they turned up a bottle of brandy. They charged him with trespassing, carrying an open container, communicating threats, and resisting arrest.

With Real Deal's departure, poetry disappeared from the green-boards and early morning hours at the hall became as silent and dull as a funeral home, though his absence didn't explain all of the mourning.

An economic downturn was under way, and by November day-labor jobs were growing scarcer, especially because the construction industry was facing a decline. "We are the first to be hired and the first to be fired," explained Jeffrey Burnett, CEO of Labor Finders, a national franchise operation. Headlines declared "Day Labor Jobs Drying Up" and "Construction Day Laborers Idle." Labor Ready, the nation's largest day-labor chain, reported a revenue loss of nearly 30 percent, and closed 70 of its 920 halls.

As the stock market plummeted, those on the bottom of the labor market fell first if not farther. An influx of superior workers began displacing the labor-hall regulars. These newcomers owned cars, didn't drink 211, and were skilled in various trades. "We have journeymen carpenters who made twenty dollars an hour who are hoping to make eight dollars now," a Labor Ready manager told the *Seattle Times*. "Our worker base is full of skilled people," a manager in Wisconsin said. "We've got people who owned their own business. We're doing our best. I let them know that the chances of working aren't huge."

The men and women with whom I worked were by and large people who are accustomed to living on the edge. They are now being shoved off a precipice, into a chasm with no safety net. Even they were not prepared for that.

17

CONCLUSION

The true stories that I have told demonstrate that day-labor agencies fill a useful niche in the economy, just like taxi companies; everybody needs to make temporary arrangements sometimes. But day-labor agencies are suppliers of long-term labor as well, and even as temporary suppliers, their operations are nearly anarchic. Client firms can't be sure if workers dispatched to them are law-abiding or on the lam, sober, disabled or fit. Workers don't know when they'll work or how long they must wait to find out if they will work. When they do "catch out," they often don't know what tasks they'll be assigned or how much they will be paid. Most of them get by without health insurance, and the consequences of minor injuries and bad weather are theirs to bear alone. At every turn, they're denied wages, benefits, and protections conferred on other workers, for the same or similar jobs. They rightly sense that the invisible hand of the market is picking their pockets.

Americans may take as gospel the adage "That government which governs least, governs best," but we haven't shown much enthusiasm for lawlessness. None of us want to take a chance that a taxi driver might be a paroled rapist, nor does anyone want to engage a cab with bald tires and bad brakes. Through our governments, we regulate taxi companies everywhere. The day-labor industry deserves similar oversight.

The first step in regulating the agencies is requiring them to declare their existence to the bureaucracies that monitor the labor market. The federal government doesn't supervise nonunion labor halls, and only eight states require them to register. Lobbyists are largely responsible for the "free" or unregulated character of the industry, but a lack of information is responsible too. Before activists or officials can impose order and devise laws, they need facts, a view of history, a few principles—and perhaps the will to dare.

They don't have what they need, and one consequence, I believe, is that reformers tend to blame agencies, not their client firms, for the sorry state of things. Yet the life of day laborers is even grimmer when agencies aren't on the scene, as the circumstances of street-corner day laborers show.

The Facts As We Know Them

In 2004, with funding from the Ford and Rockefeller foundations, sociologists from Los Angeles, Chicago, and New York, at the head of teams of graduate students and volunteers, interviewed some 2,660 of the mostly Latino workers who wait on street corners and outside building-supply stores for job offers. Most of them, the survey of 139 cities found, are immigrants hired for construction or landscaping projects. The study's thirty-two-page report, published in 2006 as *On the Corner: Day Labor in the United States* found that:

> On any given day, approximately 117,600 [street corner] workers are either looking for day-labor jobs or working as day laborers.... Median earnings during peak periods (good months) are $1,400, while in slow periods (bad months) median monthly earnings fall to just $500.

But because they work in an entirely "free" and unmediated environment, even their wages aren't guaranteed. "Almost half of all day laborers," the study reported, "experienced at least one instance of wage theft in the two months prior to being surveyed." Employers frequently engage them, drive them to a work site, and when the job is done, on the pretext of going to an ATM machine to get payroll cash, abandon them without so much as providing bus fare home.

Construction work is inherently hazardous, and the street-corner market is relatively "free" from protection, the survey found:

> Workplace injuries are common. One in five day laborers has suffered a work-related injury, and more than half of those who were injured in the past year did not receive medical care. More than two-thirds of injured day laborers have lost time from work.

The study also found that when a street-corner laborer suffers a serious injury, his employer is likely to dump him at the entrance to an emergency room—and disappear. If agency day laborers see themselves as the victims of myriad pickpockets, street-corner workers suffer from something that could more nearly be called employer assault.

Much has been made in the daily press about the immigration status of the street-corner crowd. Three-quarters of those who spoke to the Ford-Rockefeller interviewers confessed that they were "undocumented immigrants," not authorized to reside or work in the United States. What the survey did not reveal was what percentage of their employers were authorized to hire them without deducting income tax or Social Security payments, without paying premiums for unemployment and workers' compensation insurance, and so on—but the probable answers are "none" and "next to none." The employers of undocumented workers are themselves undocumented.

Thanks to the Ford-Rockefeller study, we know more about the nation's immigrant day laborers than we do about the far more numerous agency workers in the aboveground labor market. No comparable study of agency laborers has been produced in years. No government office, nobody—except maybe their agency employers, for whom secrecy is a commercial necessity—can authoritatively tell us how much agency laborers are earning, how often they are injured, or how long they spend in their status as temporaries.

Even the size of the labor-hall workforce is subject to speculation. The last thorough Bureau of Labor Statistics, or BLS, report, covering figures from 2005, showed some 1.2 million "temporary help agency workers"—a category that includes office and specialized-skill temps—at work on any given day. It estimated their weekly income at $414, a figure that reflected the higher earnings of the white-collar and skilled temporaries. It also reported that only 8.3 percent of this group—including the office and specialized workers!—were covered by medical insurance. Its data could not yield figures for lost time or workplace injuries, and in the years since 2005, BLS data collection has decreased due to budget cuts.

Tables the BLS published in January 2008 estimated the number of temporary help agency workers at 2.5 million, and at 2 million at year's end, after the economy had begun its nosedive. Scholars guess that their present number is between 800,000 and 1.4 million. But the importance of agency workers is greater than their numbers because, everyone who has studied the field agrees, millions of others in the broader market that sociologists and the BLS call the "contingent labor force" are working under the same, stunted statutory regime. Many formerly salaried jobs, like those of telephone and cable installers, are now contracted and paid as piecework. Not only day laborers, but hundreds of thousands of contract workers in the clerical, medical, legal, or information technology fields—even substitute teachers—are only spottily protected by law.

In its 2005 report, the BLS estimated that as many as six million people are contingents, workers it defines as those "who do not expect their jobs to last or who reported that their jobs are temporary"—some 2 to 4 percent of the nation's workforce. Though the BLS estimate included on-call workers and independent contractors, several scholars argue that others, including "involuntary part-time workers," that is, people who want but can't find full-time jobs, should be added to the category. If they were, more than a fourth of the nation's workforce of 140 million would fit the bill.

Though the incomes and working conditions of white-collar temps and blue-collar subcontractors are more felicitous than those of agency day laborers, as University of Illinois professor Nik Theodore has observed, almost all forms of contingent employment are marked by "low wages, a high degree of worker alienation, few prospects for upward mobility and a greater degree of exploitation than in the labour market as a whole." The regulation of day labor would improve circumstances for millions of workers, but the full scope of any regulatory scheme cannot be ascertained, because the freshest statistics are five years old.

History

The father of labor agencies in the Western world was probably one of the employers who hired workers at the *agora* (marketplace) in ancient Athens, where job seekers "shaped up," or formed lines for viewing and selection. According to long-departed French classical scholar Gustave Glotz's *Ancient Greece at Work*, the background and straits of those unfortunates were similar to those of day laborers today:

> From one end of the Hellenic world to the other roamed a mass of vagabonds, tossed hither and thither by their distress or by their love of change. Besides a few runaway slaves, they were chiefly banished men and adventurers, some cast out by their family and others fleeing from a blood feud. All these men were free, but they had to work hard to defend their existence.

Among the day laborers of ancient Athens were immigrants known as Thetes. Glotz notes that in the surviving literature:

> The Thetes are mentioned with the slaves. And indeed they do the same work, and their material condition is the same, minus security for the morrow but plus the ownership of their own body. . . . Their only advantage lies in a precarious liberty.

In industrializing England, unemployed men sought jobs through "gangmasters," a term that survives in British law to designate agents who contract laborers for agricultural work. Day-labor hiring was noted on American soil in the nineteenth century, and grew to rowdy proportions on street corners and in parks in the robber baron age. Particularly notorious were the *padrones* who sent Italian immigrants into coal mines, providing them with bunks and pay when—and if—they emerged from the depths.

Employment agencies spread as an alternative to the chaos of shape-up markets, but they, too, delivered abuse. Some operated from offices in the hats of their agents, who collected fees from job seekers and sent them to work sites that didn't exist, or from which newly engaged workers were fired within days. George Gonos, a State University of New York sociologist who is the leading historian of American labor-agency law, has explained that the soon-fired workers were victims of "fee splitting," a practice in which employment agents and foremen colluded to divide the agent's take.

Abuses like fee splitting inspired a 1909 revolt in Spokane, Washington, by firebrands of the Industrial Workers of the World, and fomented crusades by Progressive reformers, culminating in federal hearings in a dozen cities between 1912 and 1915. One result of the Progressive-era agitation, Gonos notes, was that by 1928, thirty-nine states had enacted legislation requiring employment agencies to register and report, though skirmishes continued over whether the states had authority to ban or limit agency fees. Frances Perkins, who headed the Department of Labor during the presidency of Franklin D. Roosevelt, was frustrated in her efforts to subject employment agencies to federal oversight, but when the dust settled following World War II, the practice of charging fees to job seekers had largely disappeared. A half-century of scandal had brought a handful of minor reforms, but paperless hiring continued.

Law

Contemporary labor agencies had mothers as well as fathers, among them the distaff operators of an 1887 Chicago business machine. The

Comptometer was a calculator that did not utilize what we would today call a "standard" keyboard. Because operating the machine called for the simultaneous use of as many as three fingers and sometimes the deployment of both hands, in 1928 its manufacturer, in a hundred schools scattered across the nation, began conducting three-week and three-month training programs. The company placed some twenty thousand graduates with employers each year, some of them in temporary, inventory-week jobs. Comptometer's success was noted as far away as Australia, where the company ran a vigorous temporary service, and almost as soon as World War II ended, similar agencies sprouted in Chicago, Minneapolis, Detroit, and Milwaukee. One of them, Detroit's Kelly Girl, became an early model for the temp industry, whose chief business for the next twenty years was supplying clerical workers.

The burgeoning business of leasing temporary workers operated in a legal no-man's-land. Agency offices weren't mere hiring sites, as street corners, docks, or factory gates had been. Yet they weren't employers in the usual sense of the word, because they did not provide what Gonos calls the "New Deal model of employment"—jobs of indefinite duration, with pension and other benefits. Gonos cites four conditions that make "temporary help firms," or THFs, different from employers of the ordinary kind:

1. It is the "customer" or client firm that exercises direct control over the work, which is normally carried out on the client's premises and with the client's supervisory personnel in charge.
2. The worker is not technically "employed" until she begins work on the premises of the THF's client. . . .
3. The THF normally does not supply its own materials or utilize its own tools, nor does it guarantee or take responsibility for a final product or service . . .
4. The work performed by temporary workers . . . directly benefits . . . the customer or client firm, not the THF.

Initially, most states chose to regard temporary firms as employment agencies, and that hobbled them: They were required to register, to keep records of their activities, and to open their books to labor authorities.

Individually and through industry associations, in the late 1950s temporary agencies began challenging their status in courts, with mixed results. Under the leadership of Manpower, a firm that has since widely diversified and globalized, they took a new tack—lobbying. By 1971 visits with legislators had secured the revision of laws in all of the key states. The language of the changed laws and regulations declared that client companies paid for mere services, not for labor, and that the employer of temp workers was the agency, not its client firms. These revisions exempted temporary agencies from the strictures that govern employment agencies—and opened windows that client firms use to escape the usual responsibilities of employers.

"By insinuating themselves between the worksite employer and the employee," Professor Theodore and a frequent collaborator, Jamie Peck, found that "staffing companies shield firms from regulatory costs, such as exposure to unemployment insurance or workers' compensation claims, while also decoupling temporary workers from workplace benefits, such as health insurance and pension entitlements."

Workers' compensation programs make payments to people who are disabled in workplace accidents. Such programs require employers to carry insurance. As with auto insurance rates, premiums for unemployment and workers' compensation policies are generally based on "experience-rating": the more frequent the claims brought against an employer, the higher the rates.

But when labor suppliers are regarded as employers, a negligent contractor, seeing his premiums rise, may choose to lower his costs by laying off regular employees and hiring temps. If he's really deft, he may fire his employees and rehire them—the very same workers—as weekly-ticket temps.

Unemployment insurance programs, which pay jobless benefits, "act as a penalty to firms that generate unemployment, inducing employers to adopt higher-wage, lower-turnover strategies," according to Theodore and Peck. But hiring weekly-ticket workers provides an alternative that the authors of unemployment insurance legislation probably could not have foreseen. When a client firm dispenses with temporary workers, they are not deemed to have been laid off as long as their agency is willing to send them to new assignments, however fleeting those new assignments might be.

By all these means, the statutes that recognized temporary agencies as employers set up what critics call a shell game, even a money-laundering racket. By paying money to agencies rather than agency workers, employers lower their insurance premiums and such customary labor costs as vacation pay, and medical and retirement benefits. The worker who reports to a labor hall every morning, as most agency day laborers do, is an "employee" without the customary protections and benefits of a full-time job.

The conversion of employment agencies into service providers created not only opportunities to evade labor-protection traditions and laws, but courtroom quandaries as well, especially in cases involving traffic accidents. For example, if a worker is driven to his or her job in a van owned by a temporary-labor agency, and due to its driver's negligence, an accident ensues, the agency can be held liable. But if the agency dispatches Worker B to a job site in Worker A's auto and an accident results, who is legally responsible, Worker A or the agency? If a foreman instructs a temp-agency worker to load the client firm's pickup with shovels and to drive it from one work site to another, and an accident results, who can be sued, the worker, the client firm, or the agency?

The status of temp firms has also given rise to paradoxes in labor law. If regular employees decide to form a union, are weekly-ticket workers who perform the same or similar jobs eligible to vote in a union certification election? If salaried employees of a client firm have access to washrooms or break rooms, can temporary-agency workers be denied entry?

A few conflicts of law deriving from what economists call the "triangulated" agency-worker-client relationship are exotic perhaps simply because their subjects are. If a Real Deal, while riding in a comrade's car to a job site, buys two cans of 211, finishing off the second as he reports to the client firm's foreman, whom he later assaults, who pays for the foreman's broken nose? Real Deal, the labor agency, or the client firm? Judges wrestle with questions like these, but do not come up with uniform rulings.

In 2002 the General Accounting Office surveyed both agency and street-corner markets of day labor for Illinois congressman Luis V. Gutierrez. When its investigators looked into the operation of the Occupational Safety and Health Act (OSH), and the Occupational Safety and Health Administration (OSHA), they found that "the responsibilities of temporary staffing agencies under the OSH are unclear . . . because when employers record an injury, they are not required to note whether the worker was a day laborer." They reported that "because client employers—not temporary staffing agencies—must record injuries and fatalities . . . the data OSHA uses cannot identify the extent to which day laborers working for temporary staffing agencies are injured or killed." They also found that "almost one-third of temporary staffing agencies were not in compliance with FLSA [the Fair Labor Standards Act]" and that the "FLSA provides [the federal Department of] Labor with no authority to assess penalties for failure to keep accurate payroll records."

The triangulated employee-employer relationships created by temporary agencies produce brainteasers and statistical chasms, and open loopholes in existing regulations. Statutory and bureaucratic reform would cut through a thousand Gordian knots.

Reform

When facts are in short supply, theories and principles come into play. When we're lucky, they accord with the parameters of the unknown and bring happy results, but when we're unlucky—as has been the case in most efforts to reform the day-labor industry—they produce results that are counterproductive or pointless.

Day-labor halls are practically foreign turf for highly literate people, those who clamor for and write new laws. Like pawnshops and bail-bond offices, they have acquired shady reputations largely because most of the people who patronize them are down-at-the-heels and more than a few are felons. What might be called drive-by research easily persuades the uninitiated that day-labor agencies are untrustworthy. "The physical appearance, geographic location and business names of these inner-city hiring halls point unambiguously to their function as traders of minimally processed labor-power," Professor Theodore and collaborator Chirag Mehta noted in a description of Chicago's three hundred blue-collar temp firms. The halls, they continued,

> typically occupy run-down storefronts, often with boarded windows. The interior décor is Spartan and often shabby, with uncarpeted floors and hard benches or plastic seats, designed for waiting around for job orders to be dispatched through a window to the office in the back. And typical business names are appropriately literal—Labor World, Ready Men, Temps Unlimited, World of Temps, Good Workers, Inc., Minutemen, Days & Nights, Flash Employment, Laborama, and irony surely unintended, Labor Power, Inc.

Because the look and patronage of day-labor halls, like that of many pawnshops, is of marginality and desperation, well-meaning reformers assume that the businesspeople who operate them are likely to be shady too. They have therefore focused their efforts on hiring halls rather than on the client firms that hire day laborers—or on the greater economic maladies in which labor halls nest.

An example of beside-the-point reform is a November 2006 ruling by a New York appeals court in a case brought by the state's attorney general. The court's finding altered procedures for paying workers in the state's branches of Labor Ready, the nation's largest blue-collar temp firm.

Workers at Labor Ready halls in all states but New York and Arizona, where a similar "reform" was implemented, are today offered two ways to receive their wages—by check, or by vouchers that can be cashed only at machines in Labor Ready halls. The company's cash-dispensing machines (CDMs in the language of the court) take a cut from wages: all monies of less than one dollar, plus a dollar for good measure. For example, if a worker earns $51.84, when he or she enters a unique code number on a machine's keyboard, it will deliver $50 instead. According to news stories accompanying the New York decision, Labor Ready grossed some $8 million in revenue from the machines its branches provided in 2005.

The New York court found that the state's existing labor regulations allowed payroll deductions not required by governments only when such deductions were made "for the benefit of the employee." The state's regulations did not list ready cash as a benefit.

Labor Ready argued that the dollar-plus charges were a fee justified by the cost of owning and maintaining the machines, but the company's attorneys could not persuade the judges, who ruled that "since the voucher already has the fee subtracted and can be cashed only at a Labor Ready CDM, the deduction is not disconnected from the payment of wages."

The irony of the verdict, which perhaps lay beyond the street savvy of the solons, is that many day laborers do not have bank accounts; most need money immediately—and check-cashing firms charge two to three dollars per transaction. Besides that, the bars, groceries, and commercial firms that turn checks into cash often lie blocks away. Reaching them requires a walk, sometimes in inclement weather, or a drive—in cars that many day laborers don't have.

Over the past ten years, in nearly two dozen states, some seventy-five "worker centers" have arisen as the fruit of a movement to protect immigrant street-corner workers. But the movement's success has been incomplete and underwhelming. Its most common result has been to put roofs over the heads, and commodes beneath the butts, of street-corner workers as they wait for jobs. Worker centers have been promoted not only by immigrant-rights advocates, but also by activists for neighborhood associations, whose members typically don't want day laborers defecating in their front yards. Municipal governments have acceded to, even funded, construction of the centers, largely because police officers frequently have to contend with traffic jams on corners where workers and employers congregate, and also because they must resolve complaints from merchants who, on rainy days, complain about workers "loitering" in their stores.

Labor unions have reluctantly given a nod, especially when the centers require employers to sign registries when hiring. A few worker centers attempt to enforce wage standards, but enforcing such pledges is difficult in an off-the-books labor market.

Today's worker centers are successors to nonprofit labor halls. But the record of the long-standing nonprofit halls I've been able to locate—Seattle's Millionair Club, Tucson's Primavera WORKS, and Chicago's Harbor Quest—has been one of only partial, even frustrated success. The Millionair Club, founded in 1921, dispatches more than fifty workers per day, most of them to homeowners. But like the immigrant worker centers, it does not bill employers for wages, insurance, or taxes, leaving those to negotiations between the workers and their clients.

Karen Caldwell, who oversees Primavera WORKS, a program that also operates a shelter for the homeless, says that on big jobs her business can't compete with the city's commercial labor halls because they "tend to give discounts to high-volume customers." Price-cutting by commercial firms has limited Primavera to paying its workers only pennies above the Arizona minimum wage, and to a clientele that, as with the Millionair Club, largely consists of householders.

Chicago's Harbor Quest, a hall founded in a highly industrial setting in 1970, has backed away from the day-labor operations that gave it a start to concentrate on job training, chiefly because its activists found that breaking even financially was difficult, given what its operators found to be the slim margins of commercial halls.

The financial performance of for-profit day-labor suppliers is not a matter of public record, but scholars who've looked into their operations report that the "markup"—the difference between the amount they charge client firms and the amount they pay in wages—is between 30 and 40 percent. Most of that amount, they and the books of publicly traded Labor Ready show, goes to administrative overhead, income taxes, and the costs of unemployment and accident insurance. Though profits are higher in temporary firms that supply specialized trades, the agents of raw blue-collar labor apparently prosper by taking margins as low as 5 percent on a high volume. Almost all of the signs point to client firms, not labor-hall operators, as the principal beneficiaries of low day-labor wages.

Day laborers could unionize to improve their lot, but community and labor organizers have not met with any definitive success. Both external and internal factors stand in the way.

Divisions are sharp and the ground is always shifting in the ranks of day laborers. Many part-timers look at their agency jobs as a hobby, not as bread and butter, and are therefore wary of union dues. And turnover is enough to discourage organization of any kind: A worker who became shop steward today might leave for a permanent job tomorrow, and if he didn't, many of the rank-and-filers would disappear before any election to certify a union could be held. Labor union officials would have to perpetually organize.

Another obstacle is that no Walmart, IBM, American Airlines, or even county superintendent of schools exists in the temp industry, which by the best estimates consists of some 20,000 agencies and offices. While the halls of a half-dozen national chains and franchise operations—Labor Ready, Adecco, Volt, Labor Finders, Able Body, and so on—compete in every metropolis, they face competition from a legion of mom-and-pop operators whose presence, Theodore and Mehta point out, confirms "the industry lore that start-up investments barely exceed the costs of a phone and a Rolodex."

Mom-and-pop halls easily establish themselves in niches of the market. A longtime general contractor may retire, opening a labor hall to call in chips from former subcontractors. A building materials or turf supplier may go into the business to serve longtime customers. Men and women with political connections open agencies to wheedle contracts from cronies in state, county, and municipal governments. Possibilities for capturing a slice of the market are nearly endless.

Mom-and-pop agencies perhaps exert a downward pressure on wages and profits, but their operators argue—and I know of no evidence to refute the claim—that it's the bigger companies who dominate. In any case, as my coworkers assured me many times, wages are "the same, the same everywhere," and my experience at a half-dozen halls confirms the claim. Laborers tend to pick their halls not by penny-ante wage differentials, but by location. They report to the halls nearest their homes.

Competition between labor agencies in every metropolis is a formidable obstacle to union campaigns. Organizing one labor hall is futile. Even if a majority of the workers in a city signed union cards, given the absence of registration and reporting requirements, new, nonunion halls would open their doors overnight. Organizers have unionized splintered workplaces before, it is true, in the trucking industry, for example. But their efforts, when victorious, were frequently owed as much to goon squads and arsonists as to disciplined organization.

While any hope that day laborers might improve their lot is dim, collateral parties could and may bring order to the industry's anarchy, even without having that purpose in mind. The key to such developments is not anything unique to day labor. Instead, it lies in the common interests of everyone who has a boss, in the presumptive American faith in the rule of law, and even in our fondness for weekends.

The obvious first candidate for imposing order and improvement is any system that would at last confer free and universal health care upon the American people—a measure that most voters have long favored for reasons of their own, despite the determined resistance of health care's profit takers and the cowardice or corruption of our elected leaders. Day laborers, as a rule, do not pay for health care, nor, because their incomes are low, do they pay a great deal of money into federal or state income tax systems. They go to emergency rooms for medical treatment, at great cost to the rest of us. This expense would ostensibly be reduced even under universal health care plans because emergency-room treatment is more costly than clinical care. But the chief improvement would come through the labor market, not the health-care market.

Overtime hours for regular employees have become common, just as hiring temporary workers has, in part to minimize the costs of medical care. Today it is usually cheaper, for example, to hire four workers for fifty-hour weeks than to hire five workers for forty-hour weeks, or to hire four workers for a forty-hour week, plus one temp. The contortions caused by the private provision of health care are especially painful in export industries because manufacturers in countries that already provide national health care can take advantage of what, from a purely free-market point of view, might be called "subsidized labor costs," the costs of health insurance. Were our government to take a major role in financing health care, an immediate effect would be that companies would have an incentive to hire temps onto their permanent payrolls. And with their earnings as full-fledged employees, former day laborers would be able to make a greater contribution to the costs of their medical care.

Any wave of hiring day laborers onto regular payrolls, of course, would reduce the incomes of workers who are already permanent employees by trimming their hours of overtime pay. But at some point, it seems to me that the nation must ask itself if it only wants to thunder about "family values"—or observe them. Workers who consistently clock more than forty hours a week may provide additional comfort or security to their families, but every hour of overtime work is an hour less of parenting. Income lost from overtime hours could be replaced, too, if workers rekindled their ardor for unions, which truly earned their members the title that bumper stickers bestow on them: "The Folks Who Brought You the Weekend."

Increased unionization of the permanent workforce would likely bring another benefit to day laborers and even to the agencies that employ them. Any reinvigorated union movement would attempt to curtail off-the-books arrangements, which reduce both the clientele of labor agencies and the wages of their workers. Enforcement would be simple: Undercover agents, using standard vice-squad techniques, could join shape-up ranks, accept jobs, and after shoveling a spade or two of dirt, cite or—with stiffer laws—even arrest their employers. The rationale that punishes "consensual crimes" may be dubious, but while it stands, only an outdated Puritanism can justify its application to prostitutes and drug dealers while exempting exploiters of labor.

Of course, any crusade to penalize off-the-books employers would crimp companies in the construction, landscaping, manufacturing, and food service industries, in which undocumented immigrants play a big role. But permitting immigrants to work while denying them citizenship favors only those rogue employers who don't want to face the political consequences of exploiting their workers. One of the lessons of the segregation era is that ordinary working people can't improve their circumstances by legal, peaceful, and incremental means when a great number of them are disenfranchised.

Since the financial crash of 2008, Republican pundits have variously assailed "European socialism" as part of any plan for American recovery, but that hasn't stopped policy wonks from looking across the Atlantic for ideas. They might do well to look at European day-labor reforms. Following 1935 and 1949 resolutions by the International Labor Organization, a UN-affiliated group whose origins date to the old League of Nations, and under the risible slogan that "labor is not a commodity," several European nations prohibited temporary-labor services. But in the name of a more "flexible" workforce, the ban was dismantled in country after country, as early as 1972 in France. In 1997, the ILO adopted a new standard, broadly legalizing temporary agencies—but under principles common to "European socialism." As a scholar at the Sorbonne explained in 2005, under the terms now operative in France, "the activity of hiring temporary workers is not a free business."

Two provisions are key to the regulatory regimes that have emerged in Europe. The first is a requirement for agency registration and reporting, a measure long overdue in the United States. Mandatory licensing makes possible the second and more important reform, a "parity" wage. Inserted into European legislation (even in England!) by the clout of union federations, parity wage provisions require labor halls to pay temporary workers an hourly rate not less than that of the regular employees of the firm whose workers they supplement or replace. When temps are truly hired for one-off tasks, parity regulations mandate payment of the average wage for similar work. If American authorities were to adopt a parity standard, the wages of blue-collar day laborers would nearly double.

The new European standards have not forestalled the growth of temporary-labor firms; on the contrary, business has boomed. A 2007

press bulletin of the chief trade association, the European Confedera-
tion of Private Employment Agencies, or Eurociett, proclaims that,
"Private employment agencies are . . . currently employing 3.3 million agency workers (full time equivalent) across Europe. Continued
structural growth will raise this by 1.6 million to reach 4.98 million
by 2012." Indeed, so hardy is the industry that Eurociett promotional
literature is seasoned with phrases like "labor market flexibility should
not be achieved at the detriment of workers" and with declarations like
"Representing a well-regulated industry, members of Eurociett refuse
to compete at the expense of workers' rights and work hand-in-hand
with governments to fight illegal work and social dumping."

The notion that workers—some of whom cannot, or do not, want to
work every day—should be paid hourly wages on par with regular employees perhaps grates on the "American work ethic." But if it does, that
can only be because our "work ethic" is a profit ethic, a wolf in sheep's
clothing: The purpose of the European standard is not to enrich day
laborers but to preempt the conversion of regular jobs into temp jobs.
It does as much by transferring the burden of "temporary" labor needs
from workers to profit-takers. As much as Americans may dislike adopt-
ing a similar "socialist" standard, we have already accepted it in daily
practice: When we hire taxis or rental cars, we expect to pay a premium
above the cost of driving our own cars.

But the ultimate and most important reason why Americans should
adopt European-style regulation comes to us in warnings not from Europe, but from Japan.

Figures for contingent employment in the United States show
nearly a sixfold increase since 1971, when the industry came into its
own. But its growth has not been steady. The opening of new sectors
of the market—in information technology, for example—has played a
part. But so too have economic slumps. The industry grew faster than
the job market as a whole during the recovery from the savings-and-
loan and stock market collapses of the late 1980s, and again when the
nation pulled itself out of the dot-com crash of 2000–2001. One of the
industry's characteristics, Professors Peck and Theodore report, "has
been an impressive ability to recover ever more robustly from each

downturn, sustaining increasingly long phases of growth and diversifi-cation in each successive upswing."

Indeed, contingent employment shows what might be called a ratch-eting effect, in which after each downturn, the industry gains ground, taking a bigger bite of the job pie, increasing its market share. The same pattern is stunningly evident in Japan. Twenty years ago, when its econ-omy was at its height, the Land of the Rising Sun was renowned for its practice of lifetime, layoff-less employment. When manufacturers hit a slump, instead of issuing pink slips, they ordered employees to report—to do nothing and to get paid for it. But the Japanese banking crisis of the early nineties and the ensuing "lost decade" transformed Jekyll into Hyde. No longer the home of lifetime employment, Japan became a na-tion in which a third of the workforce can find only contingent jobs.

The temp industry will likely ratchet upward at the end of the current recession, and already, editorialists of the business press are applauding its gain. A "leader," or editorial, in a recent issue of the newsweekly *The Economist* put it this way:

> Over the next couple of years, politicians will have to perform a diffi-cult policy U-turn; for in the long term, they need flexible labor mar-kets. That will mean abolishing job-subsidy programs, taking away protected workers' privileges and making it easier for businesses to restructure by laying people off. Countries such as Japan, with two-tier workforces in which an army of temporary workers with few protections toil alongside mollycoddled folk with many, will need to narrow that disparity by making the latter easier to fire.

Or in other words, as long as a gap exists between the earnings and benefits of regular employees and temps, that gap can be closed in two ways: by improving the lot of temporary workers, or by diminishing the benefits and earnings of the "mollycoddled folk," that is, the per-manently employed.

These circumstances leave those of us in the regular employment market no option. Support for the interests of those in the lowest ranks of labor protects us. Ignoring them exposes us to their fate.

ACKNOWLEDGMENTS

At various times in my life I have "caught out," or found temporary jobs, at labor halls. But only once before have I written about them, in a 1993 article for a Dallas weekly then edited by Peter Elkind.

When I proposed the idea of this book to Esther Newberg, my agent, and to editor Alice Mayhew, I crossed my fingers. I didn't think anybody would see in day-labor life what I saw. My gratitude goes out first to them, for thinking that my proposal was sensible.

I was also encouraged by the faith of fellow writers Rod Davis, Robert Bryce, and Steve Davis, who looked at parts of my manuscript, even though they made me work harder. Tara Croft caught copy errors before I submitted a final draft.

Most of all, however, I feel a debt of gratitude to the men and women with whom I worked as a laborer. They help build, service, and maintain the hardware of the economy on which we all rely—yet they go unnoticed.

INDEX

ABOUT THE AUTHOR

Dick J. Reavis is a former staff writer at *Texas Monthly*. He has written about motorcycle gangs, undocumented immigrants, guerrillas, convicts, coal miners, security guards, and bankers for publications as diverse as *Soldier of Fortune* and *The Wall Street Journal*. He is a professor in the English department at North Carolina State University.

Printed in the United States
By Bookmasters